EASY GUITAR WITH NOTES & TAB

THE BEST OF *Bob Seger*

Cover photo by Brad Stanley, courtesy of Capitol Records

ISBN 978-0-634-05687-1

HAL•LEONARD® CORPORATION

7777 W. BLUEMOUND RD. P.O. BOX 13819 MILWAUKEE, WI 53213

Visit Hal Leonard Online at
www.halleonard.com

STRUM AND PICK PATTERNS

This chart contains the suggested strum and pick patterns that are referred to by number at the beginning of each song in this book. The symbols ⊓ and ∨ in the strum patterns refer to down and up strokes, respectively. The letters in the pick patterns indicate which right-hand fingers plays which strings.

p = thumb
i = index finger
m = middle finger
a = ring finger

For example; Pick Pattern 2
is played: thumb - index - middle - ring

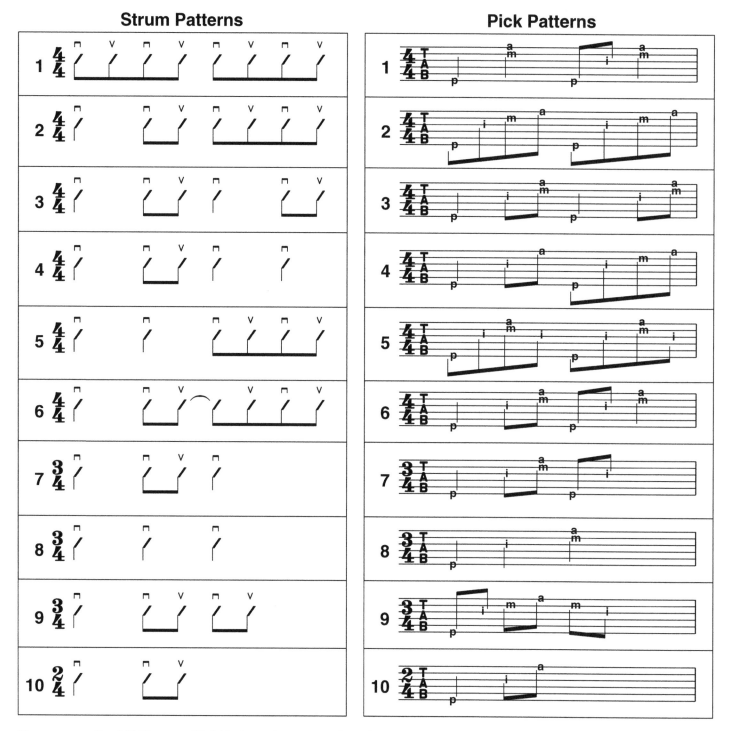

You can use the 3/4 Strum or Pick Patterns in songs written in compound meter (6/8, 9/8, 12/8, etc.). For example, you can accompany a song in 6/8 by playing the 3/4 pattern twice in each measure. The 4/4 Strum and Pick Patterns can be used for songs written in cut time (¢) by doubling the note time values in the patterns. Each pattern would therefore last two measures in cut time.

Beautiful Loser

Words and Music by Bob Seger

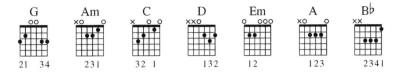

Strum Pattern: 2, 4
Pick Pattern: 4, 5

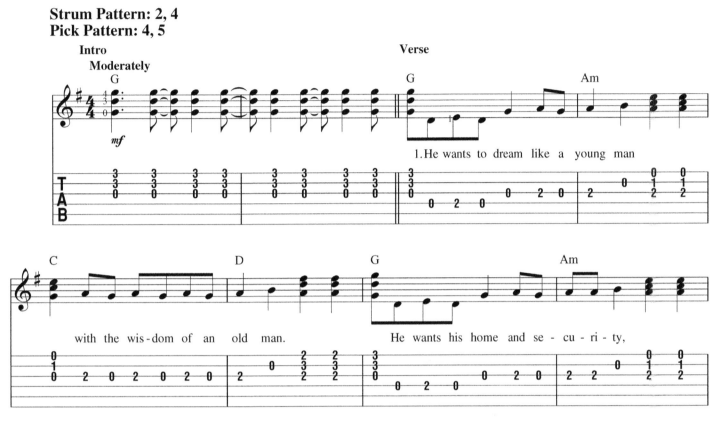

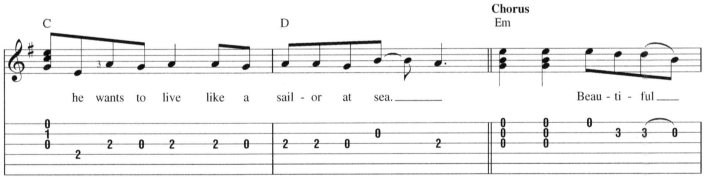

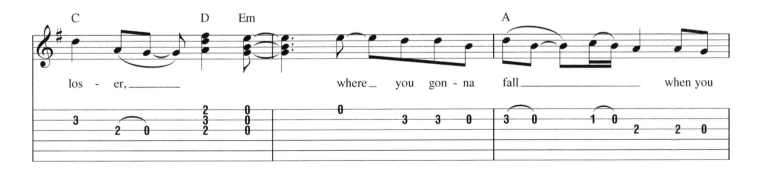

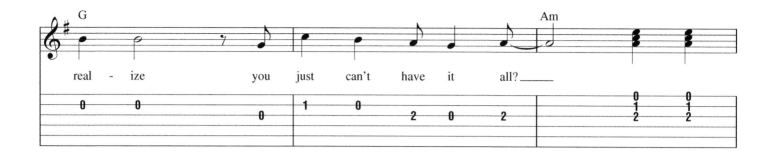

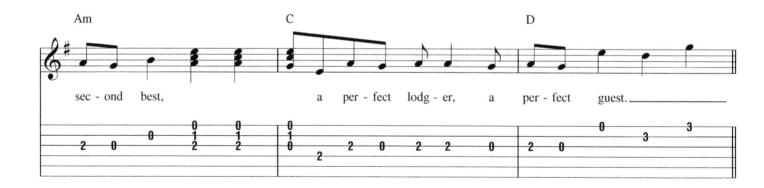

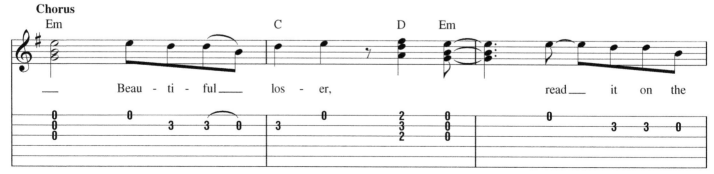

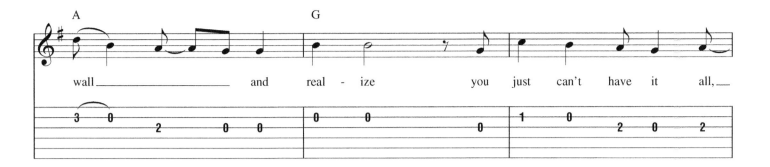

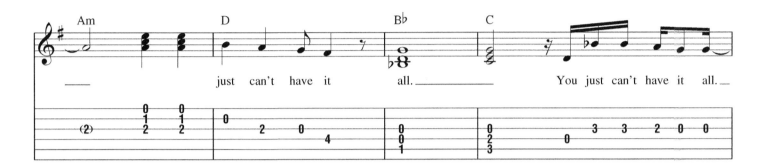

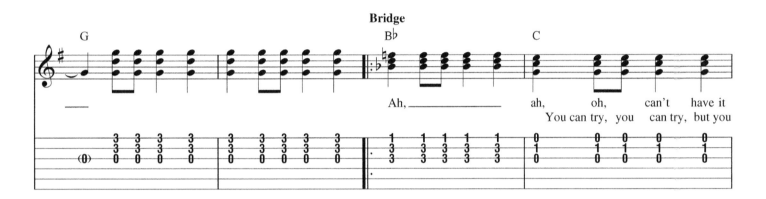

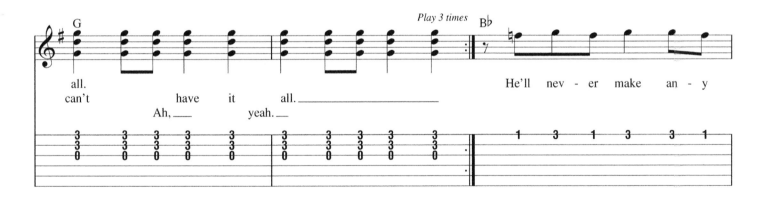

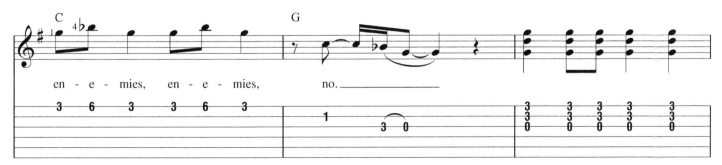

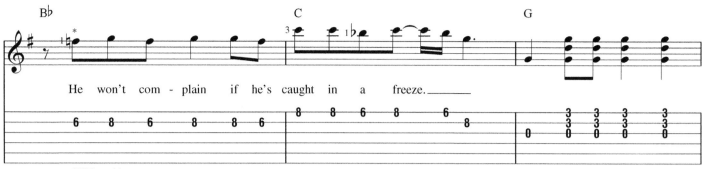

He won't com-plain if he's caught in a freeze. _____

*VIth position

He'll al - ways ask, he'll al - ways say _____ please. ____

*as before

Interlude

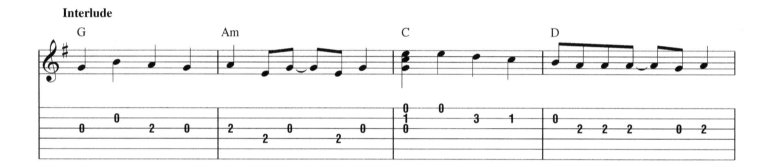

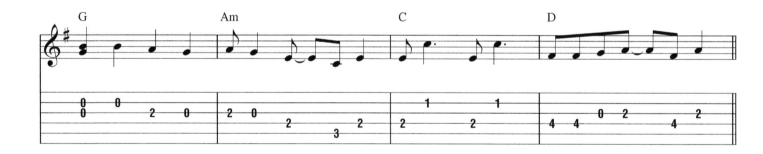

Chorus

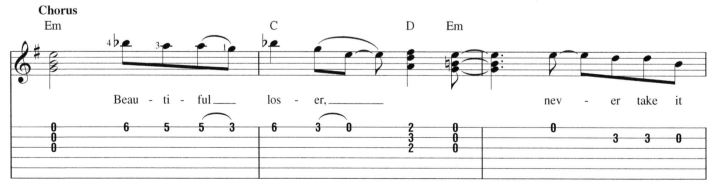

Beau - ti - ful ____ los - er, ____ nev - er take it

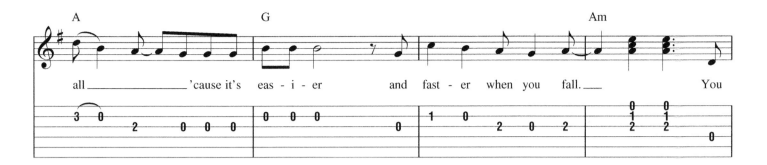

all _____ 'cause it's eas - i - er and fast - er when you fall. ____ You

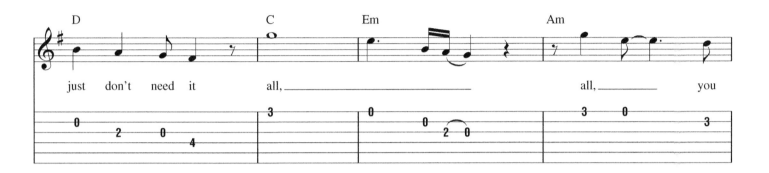

just don't need it all, _____ all, _____ you

just don't need it all. ____

Outro

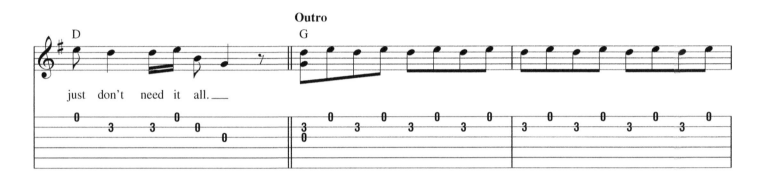

Just don't need it all. ____

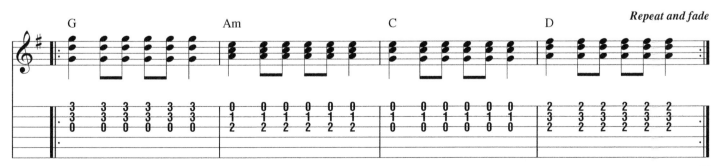

Repeat and fade

Against the Wind

Words and Music by Bob Seger

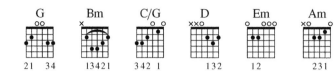

Strum Pattern: 2
Pick Pattern: 4

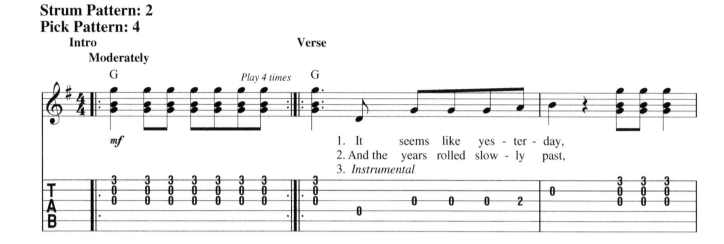

Intro
Moderately   Verse

1. It seems like yes - ter - day,
2. And the years rolled slow - ly past,
3. *Instrumental*

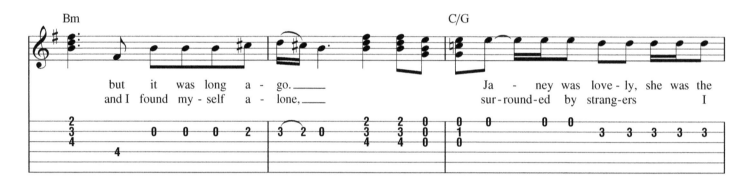

but it was long a - go._____   Ja - ney was love - ly, she was the
and I found my - self a - lone,_____   sur - round - ed by strang - ers   I

queen of my nights_____   there in the dark - ness with the
thought were my friends,_____   I found my - self fur - ther and

ra - di - o   play - ing low.__   And   and the se - crets that we
fur - ther from my ___ home.__ And I   guess I lost my

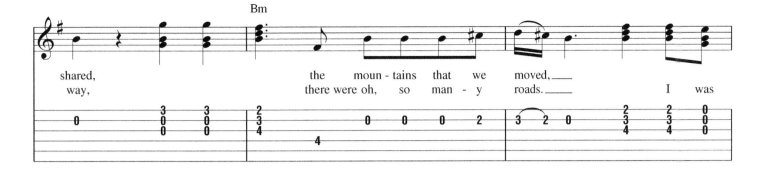

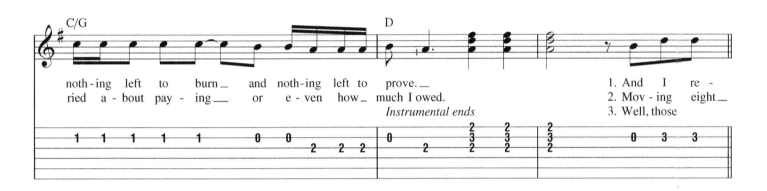

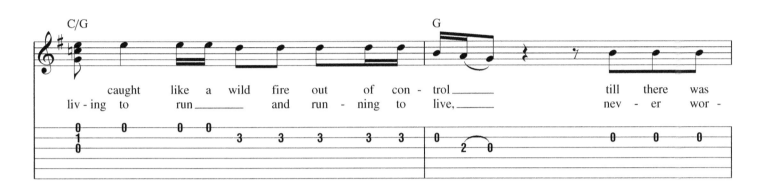

Pre-Chorus

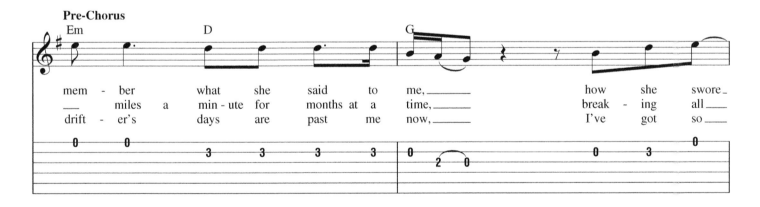

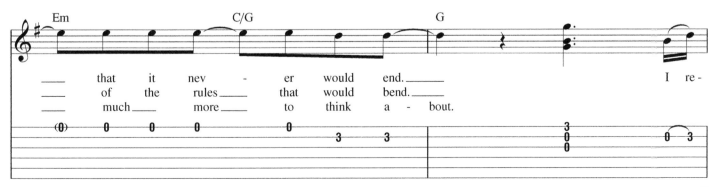

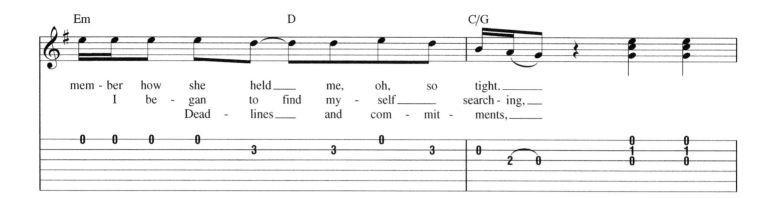

mem - ber how she held___ me, oh, so tight.___
I be - gan to find my - self___ search - ing,___
Dead - lines___ and com - mit - ments,___

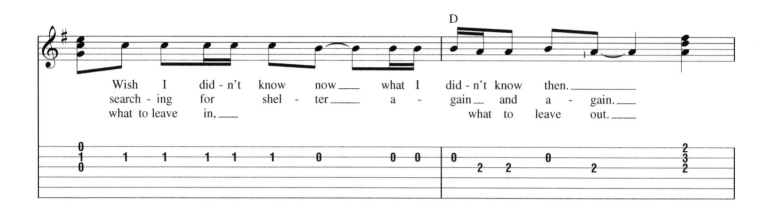

Wish I did - n't know now___ what I did - n't know then.___
search - ing for shel - ter___ a - gain__ and a - gain.___
what to leave in,___ what to leave out.___

Chorus

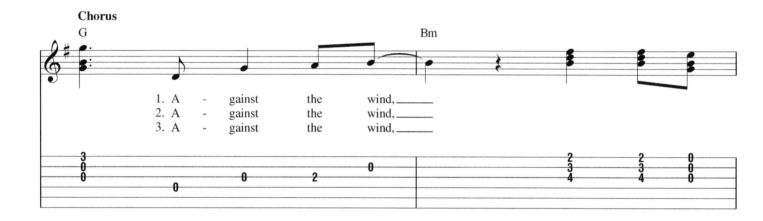

1. A - gainst the wind,___
2. A - gainst the wind,___
3. A - gainst the wind,___

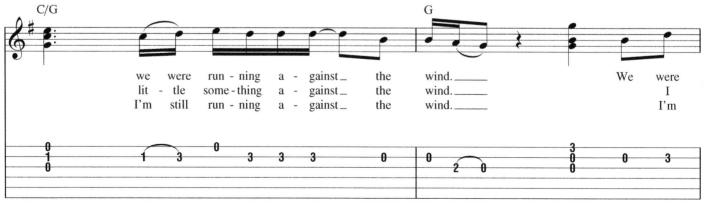

we were run - ning a - gainst_ the wind.___ We were
lit - tle some - thing a - gainst_ the wind.___ I
I'm still run - ning a - gainst_ the wind.___ I'm

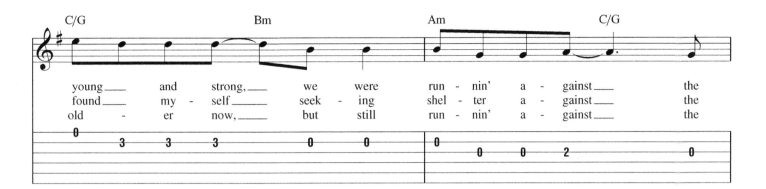

young____ and strong,____ we were run - nin' a - gainst____ the
found____ my - self____ seek - ing shel - ter a - gainst____ the
old - er now,____ but still run - nin' a - gainst____ the

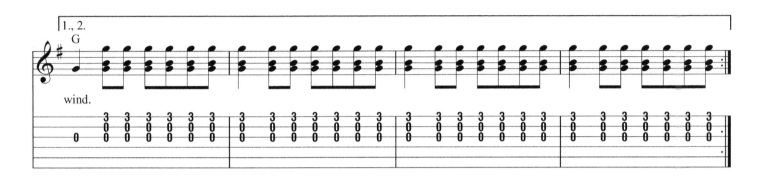

1., 2.

wind.

3.

wind.

Well, I'm old - er now__ and still

Outro

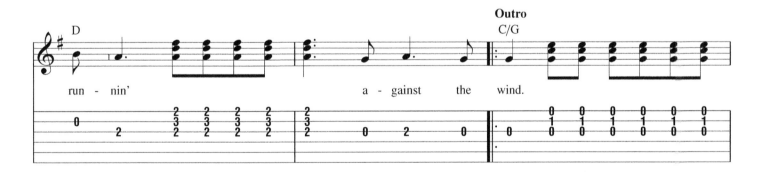

run - nin' a - gainst the wind.

Repeat and fade

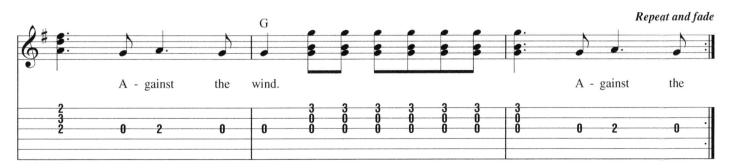

A - gainst the wind.   A - gainst the

Betty Lou's Gettin' Out Tonight

Words and Music by Bob Seger

*Capo 1

Strum Pattern: 5

*Optional: To match recording, place capo at 1st fret.

1. Have you heard the news,___ it's all o - ver town.___
2. *See additional lyrics*

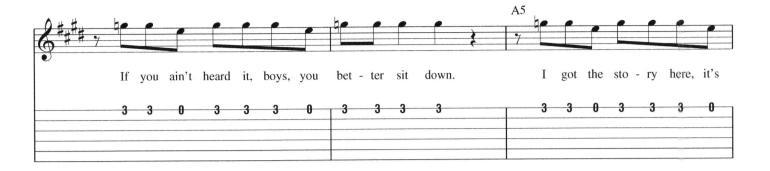

If you ain't heard it, boys, you bet - ter sit down. I got the sto - ry here, it's

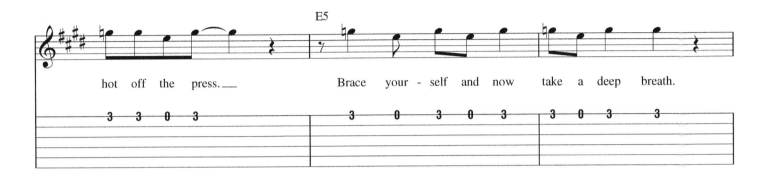

hot off the press.___ Brace your - self and now take a deep breath.

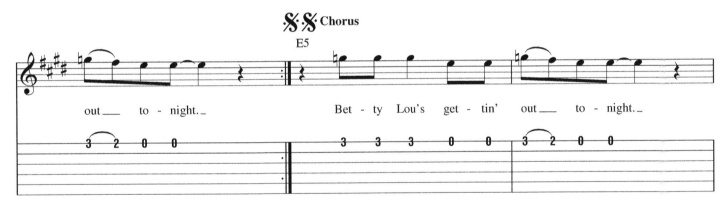

Grab a hold of some-thing, hold on tight,___ Bet - ty Lou's get - tin'

%. %. **Chorus**

out___ to - night.___ Bet - ty Lou's get - tin' out___ to - night.___

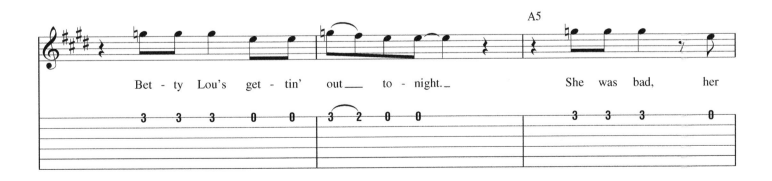

Bet - ty Lou's get - tin' out___ to - night.___ She was bad, her

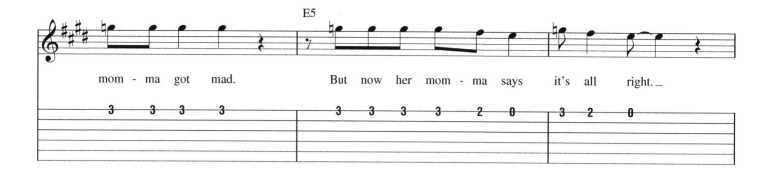

mom - ma got mad. But now her mom - ma says it's all right.__

All the boys are get - tin' read - y to ride,__ Bet - ty Lou's get - tin'

$\mathbf{\%}$ **Bridge**

To Coda 2 $\oplus$

out__ to - night.__ Bet - ty Lou.

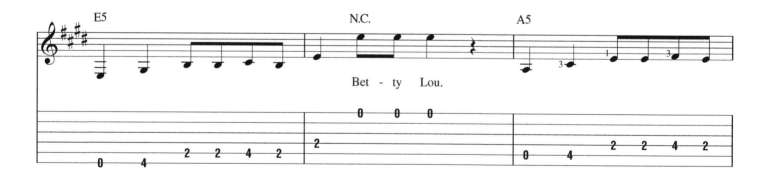

Bet - ty Lou.

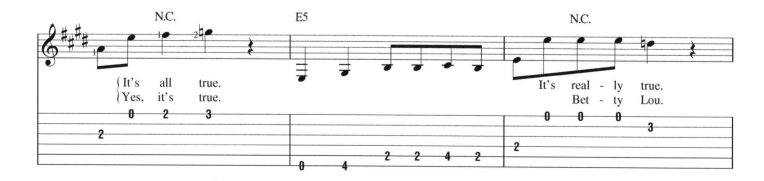

It's all true.
Yes, it's true. It's real - ly true.
Bet - ty Lou.

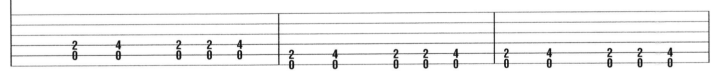

Yelled: What do you think about that boys?

Uh,   uh.

Instrumental

2nd time, D. S. al Coda 1

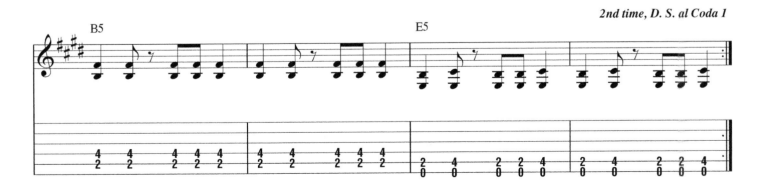

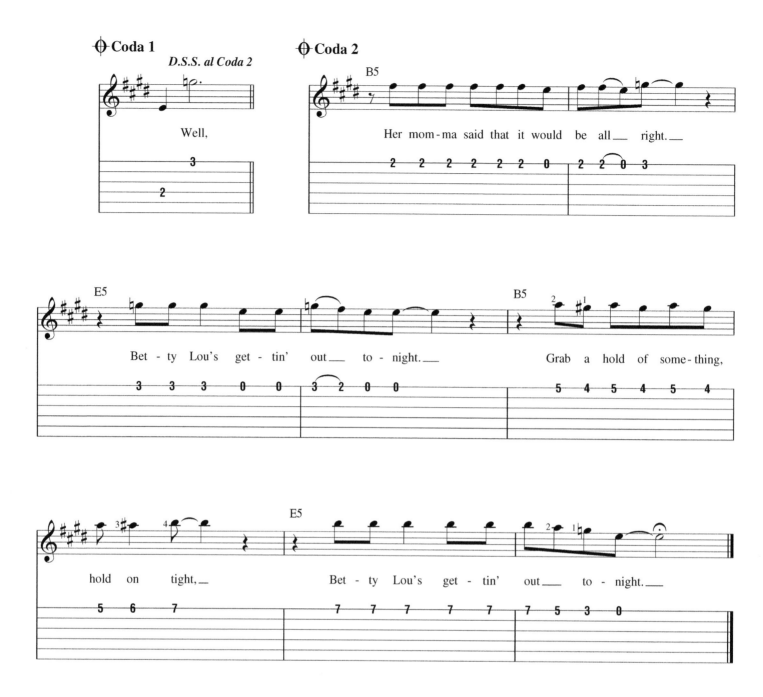

Additional Lyrics

2. First heard the rumor down on 12th and Main,
   The poor druggist, he was going insane.
   His stuff was sellin' out like never before,
   He finally had to up and close the store.
   All the boys are getting ready to fight,
   Betty Lou's gettin' out tonight.

Even Now
Words and Music by Bob Seger

Strum Pattern: 1, 2
Pick Pattern: 2, 4

Intro
Moderately fast Rock

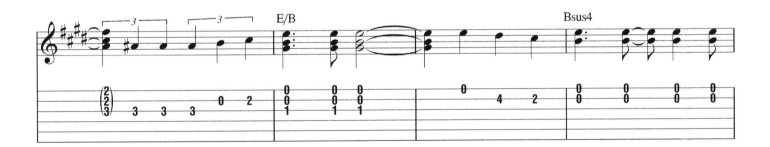

Verse

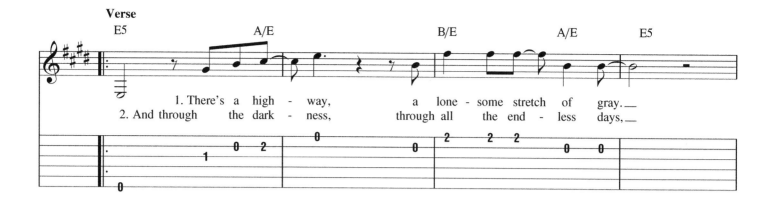

1. There's a high - way, a lone - some stretch of gray.___
2. And through the dark - ness, through all the end - less days,___

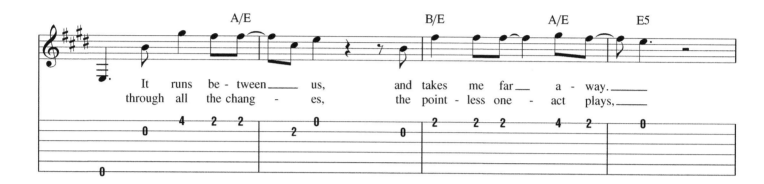

It runs be - tween___ us, and takes me far___ a - way.___
through all the chang - es, the point - less one - act plays,___

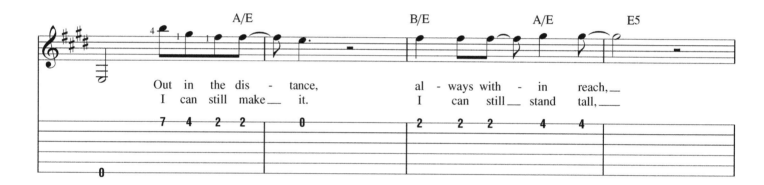

Out in the dis - tance, al - ways with - in reach,___
I can still make___ it. I can still___ stand tall,___

there's a cross - road where all the vic - tims meet.___ I
'cause I got___ my___ girl to get me through it all;___ through

Pre-Chorus

close my eyes___ and see her face. It's all I want___ to see.___ And
all the doubt___ and all the fear and all that I___ can't say.

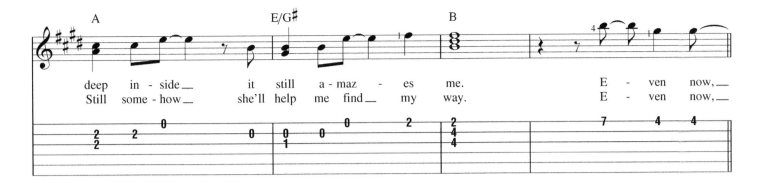

deep in - side__ it still a - maz - es me. E - ven now,__
Still some - how__ she'll help me find__ my way. E - ven now,__

Chorus

she's all that I want,__ she's all that I need. E - ven
she's still in my heart, she's still in my soul. E - ven

now,_____ she's giv - in' it all,__ she's giv - in' it free. E - ven
now,_____ she's still on my mind__ wher - ev - er I go. E - ven

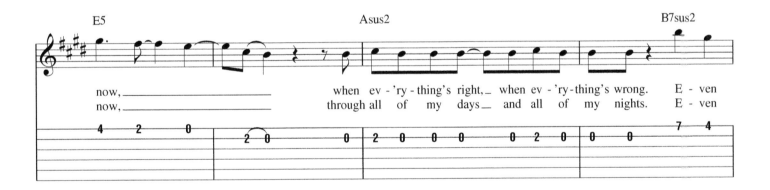

now,_____ when ev - 'ry - thing's right,__ when ev - 'ry - thing's wrong. E - ven
now,_____ through all of my days__ and all of my nights. E - ven

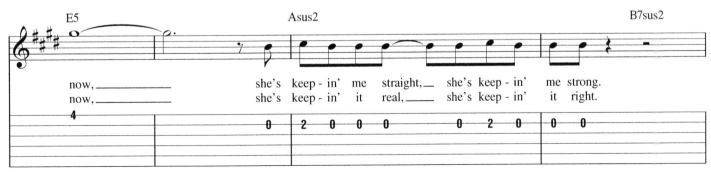

now,_____ she's keep - in' me straight,__ she's keep - in' me strong.
now,_____ she's keep - in' it real,____ she's keep - in' it right.

She gets to me____ some - how,_____ e - ven now.

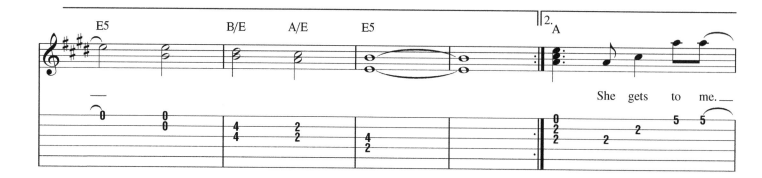

She gets to me.____

____ some - how,_____ e - ven now._____

Interlude

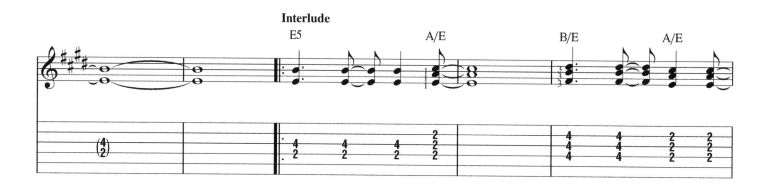

E - ven now.

She's
When

all that I want,_ she's all that I need. E - ven now,_____ she's
ev - 'ry - thing's right,_ when ev - 'ry - thing's wrong.

giv - in' it all,_ she's giv - in' it free. keep - in' it real,_ she's keep - in'

it strong.

E - ven now._____

Outro
Freely

The Fire Down Below

Words and Music by Bob Seger

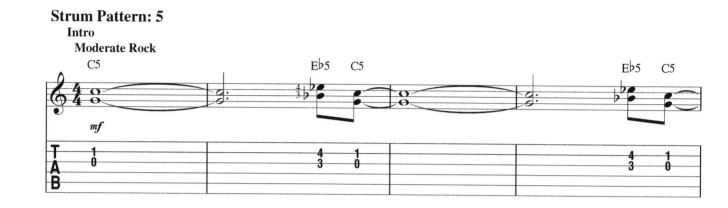

Strum Pattern: 5

Intro
Moderate Rock

1. Here comes_ old Ros - ie, she's look-in' might - y fine;_
2., 3., 5. *See additional lyrics*
4. *Instrumental*

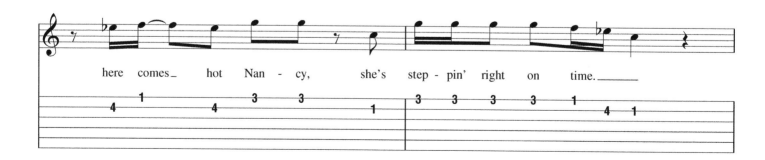

here comes_ hot Nan - cy, she's step-pin' right on time.____

There go ___ the street lights, bring - ing on the night; ___

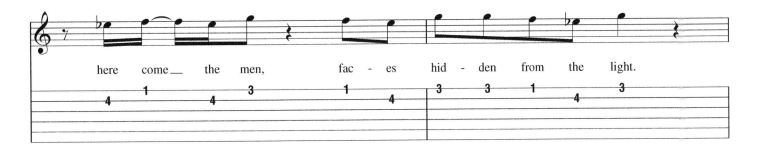

here come ___ the men, fac - es hid - den from the light.

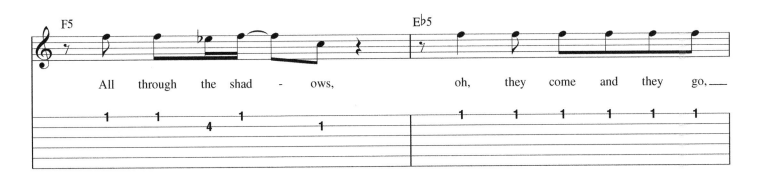

All through the shad - ows, oh, they come and they go, ___

with on - ly one ___

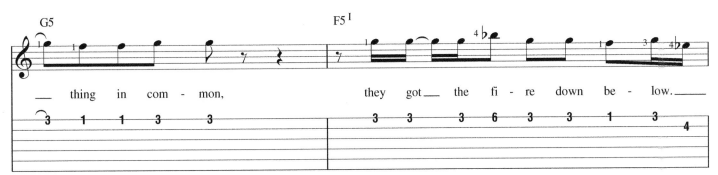

___ thing in com - mon, they got ___ the fi - re down be - low. ___

5th time, To Coda ⊕

Yeah, it

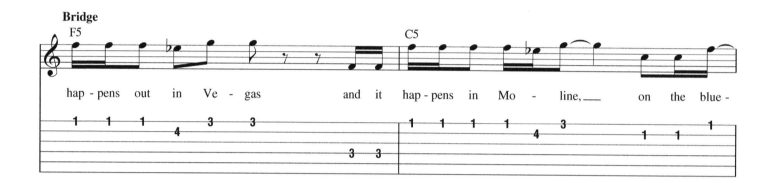

Bridge

hap - pens out in Ve - gas and it hap - pens in Mo - line,___ on the blue -

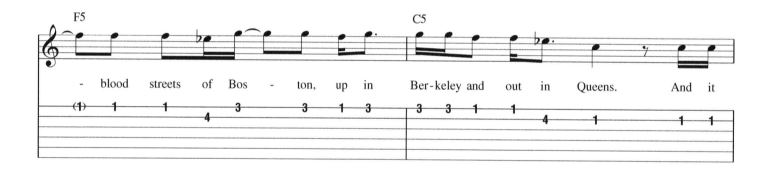

- blood streets of Bos - ton, up in Ber - keley and out in Queens. And it

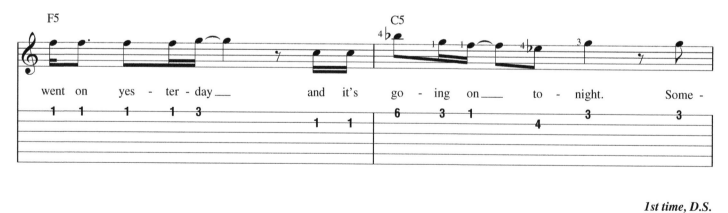

went on yes - ter - day___ and it's go - ing on___ to - night. Some -

1st time, D.S.
(take repeat)
2nd time, D.S. al Coda

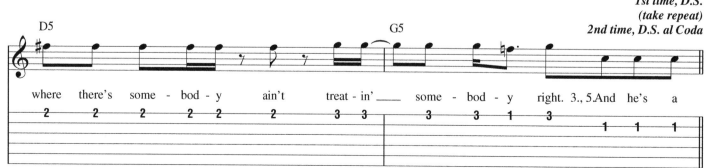

where there's some - bod - y ain't treat - in'___ some - bod - y right. 3., 5.And he's a

Coda

On - ly got one____ thing in com - mon, they got__ the fi - re down be - low.____

On - ly__ got one____ thing in com - mon,

they got the fi - re down be - low.____

Outro

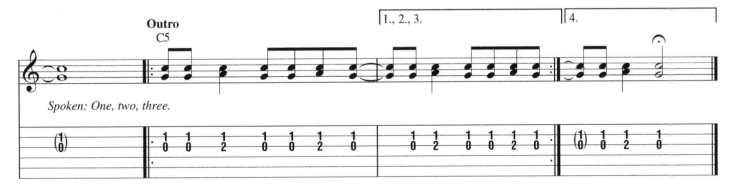

Spoken: One, two, three.

Additional Lyrics

2. Here comes the rich man
   In his big long limousine;
   Here comes the poor man,
   All you got to have is green.
   Here comes the banker
   And the lawyer and the cop;
   One thing for certain,
   It ain't never gonna stop.
   When it all gets too heavy,
   That's when they come and they go, they go,
   With only one thing in common,
   They got the fire down below.

3., 5. And he's a looking out for Rosie,
   She's looking mighty fine;
   And he's walking the streets for Nancy,
   And he'll find her ev'ry time.
   And when the street lights flicker,
   Bringing on the night,
   Well, they'll be slipping into darkness,
   Slipping out of sight.

   All through the {midnight, / shadows,}
   Watch 'em come and watch 'em go, oh, go,
   With only one thing in common,
   They got the fire down below.

Hollywood Nights

Words and Music by Bob Seger

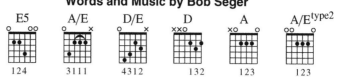

Strum Pattern: 2, 6
Pick Pattern: 4, 6

Intro
Moderately fast Rock

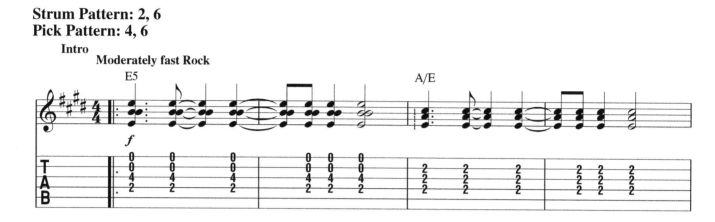

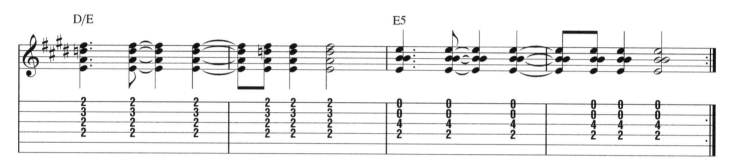

1. She stood there bright as the sun on that Cal - i - for - nia coast.
2. She took his hand and she lead him a - long that gold - en beach.
3., 4. *See additional lyrics*

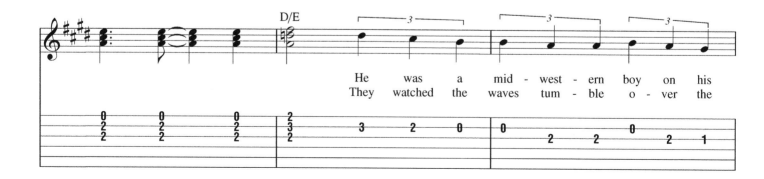

He was a mid - west - ern boy on his
They watched the waves tum - ble o - ver the

own.
sand.
She looked at him with those soft eyes, so
They drove for miles and miles___ up those

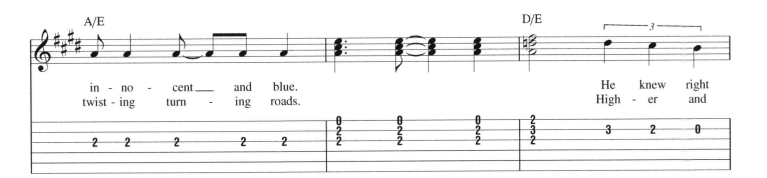

in - no - cent___ and blue.
twist - ing turn - ing roads.
He knew right
High - er and

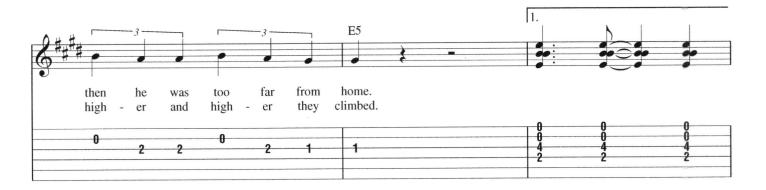

then he was too far from home.
high - er and high - er they climbed.

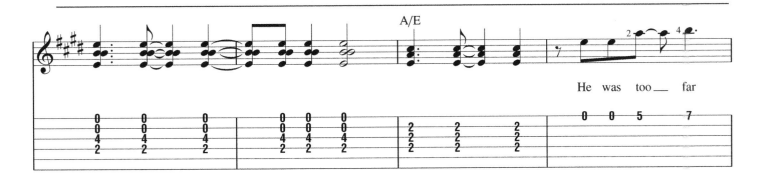

He was too___ far

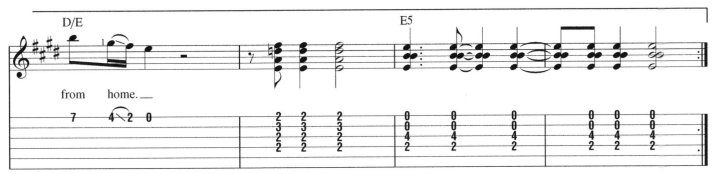

from home.___

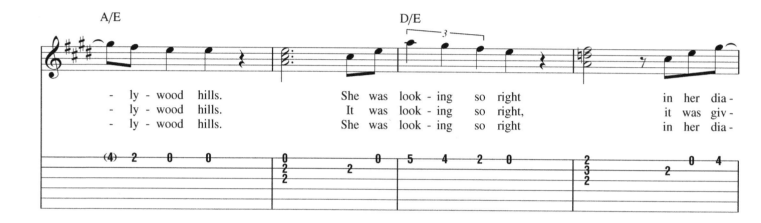

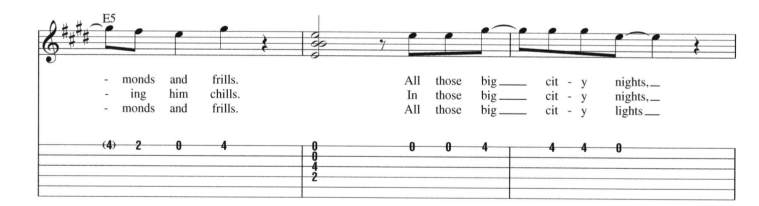

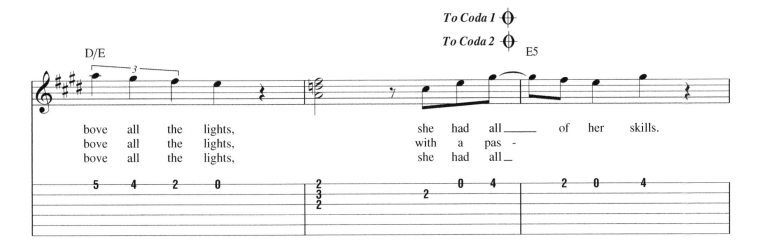

bove   all   the   lights,   she   had   all_____   of   her   skills.
bove   all   the   lights,   with   a   pas -
bove   all   the   lights,   she   had   all__

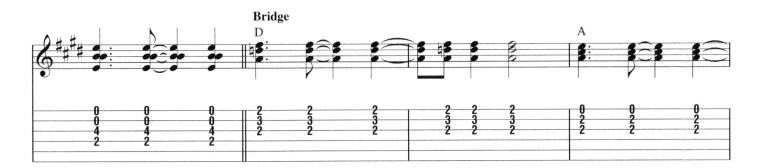

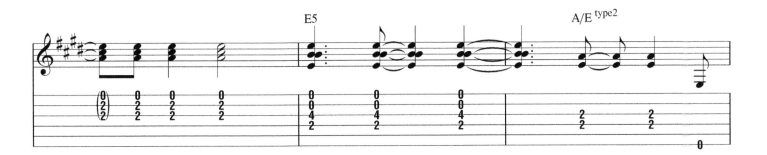

D.S. al Coda 1
(take repeat)

29

Additional Lyrics

3. He'd headed west 'cause he felt that a change would do him good.
   See some old friends; good for the soul.
   She had been born with a face that would let her get her way.
   He saw that face and he lost all control.
   He had lost all control.

4. Night after night and day after day it went on and on.
   Then came that morning he woke up alone.
   He spent all night staring down at the lights of L.A.,
   Wondering if he could ever go home.

Like a Rock

Words and Music by Bob Seger

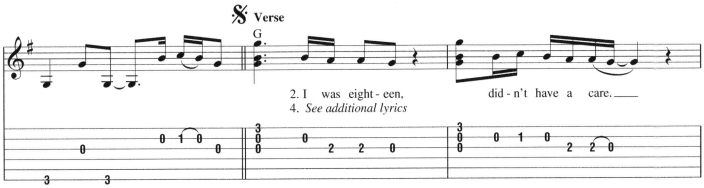

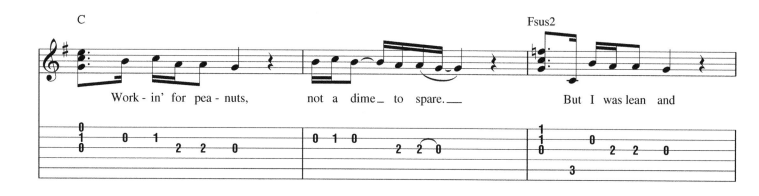

Work - in' for pea - nuts, not a dime_ to spare._ But I was lean and

sol - id ev -'ry - where,_ like a rock.

Verse

3. My hands were stead - y, my eyes were clear and bright._ My walk had pur - pose, my
5. *See additional lyrics*

To Coda ⊕

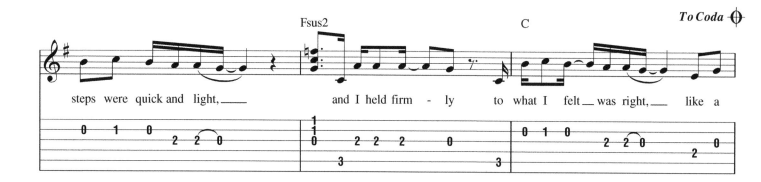

steps were quick and light,_ and I held firm - ly to what I felt_ was right,_ like a

Chorus

rock. Like a rock, I was

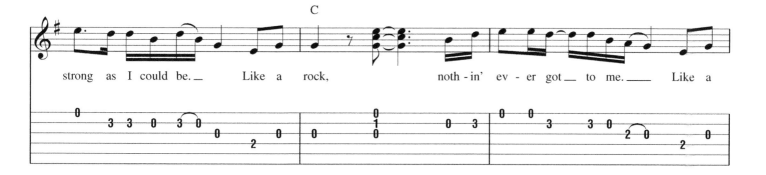

strong   as   I   could   be. _   Like   a   rock,   noth - in' ev - er got _ to me. _   Like   a

rock,   I   was some-thing   to   see, _____   like   a   rock.

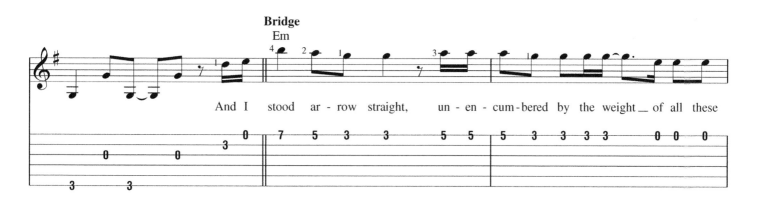

Bridge

And   I   stood   ar - row   straight,   un - en - cum - bered   by   the   weight _   of   all   these

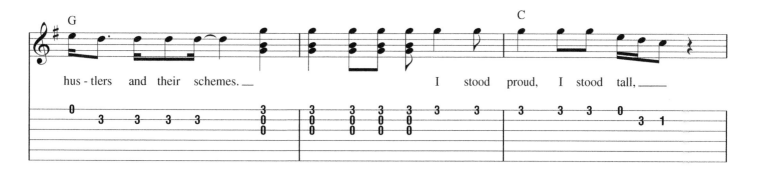

hus - tlers   and   their   schemes. _   I   stood   proud,   I   stood   tall, _____

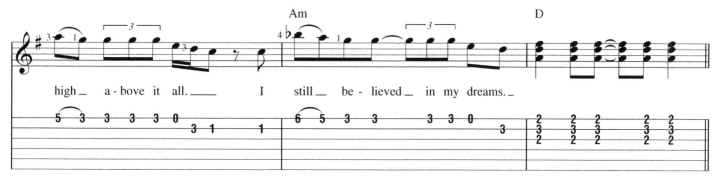

high _   a - bove   it   all. _____   I   still _   be - lieved _   in   my   dreams. _

Guitar Solo

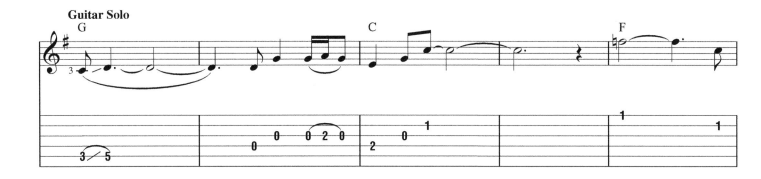

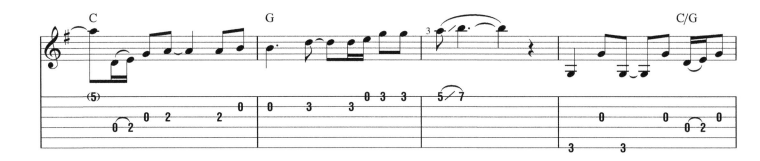

D.S. al Coda

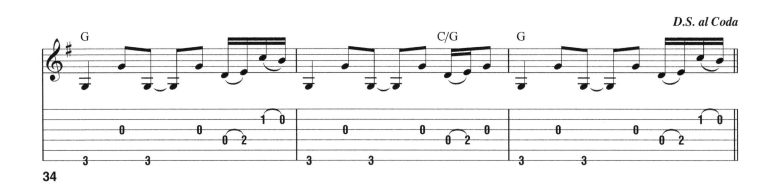

call, I re - call, like a { rock, rock, the

3rd time, Instrumental, till fade

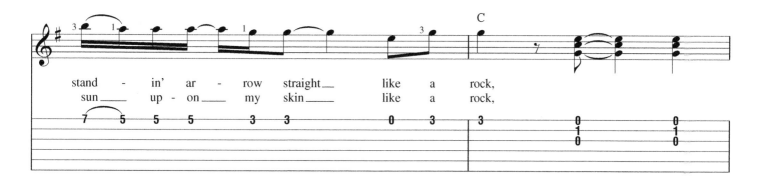

stand - in' ar - row straight___ like a rock,
sun___ up - on___ my skin___ like a rock,

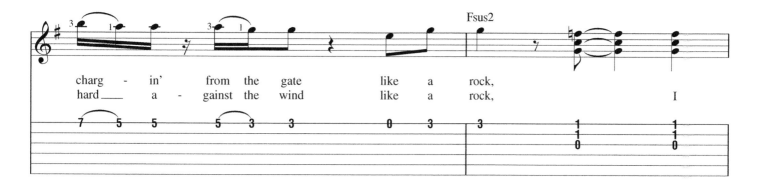

charg - in' from the gate like a rock,
hard___ a - gainst the wind like a rock, I

car - ry - in' the weight like a rock.
see my - self a - gain like a rock.

Oh, like a }
Oh, like a }

Additional Lyrics

4. Twenty years now; where'd they go?
   Twenty years, I don't know.
   I sit and I wonder sometimes
   Where they've gone.

5. And sometimes late at night,
   When I'm bathed in the firelight.
   The moon comes callin' a ghostly white,
   And I recall, I recall.

Katmandu

Words and Music by Bob Seger

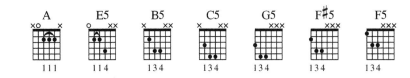

Strum Pattern: 2

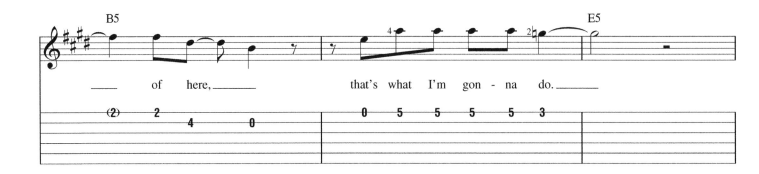

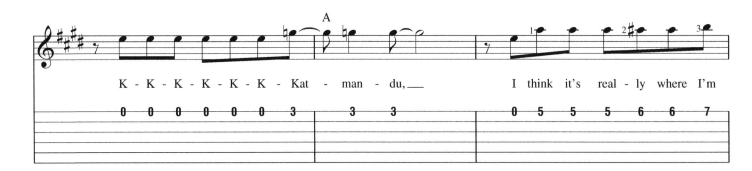

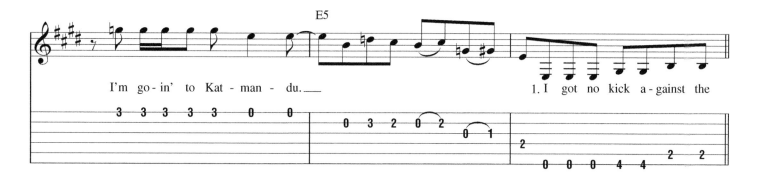

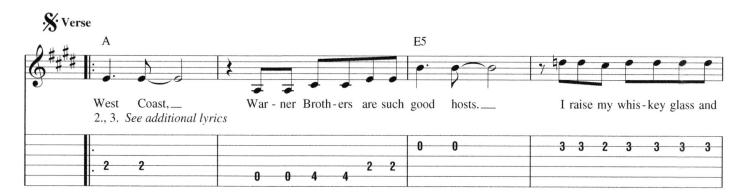

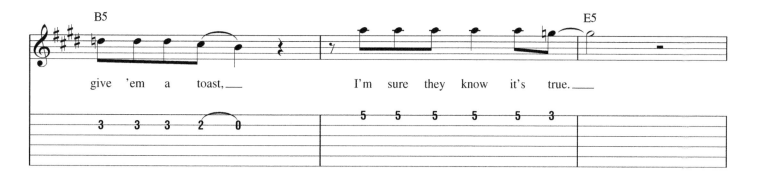

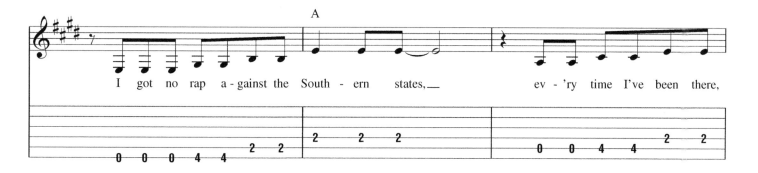

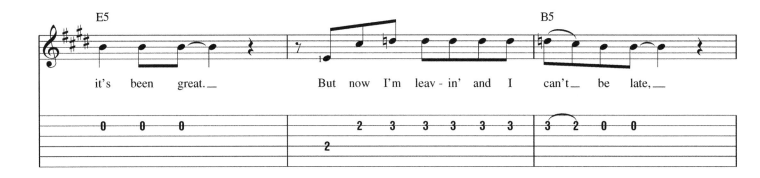

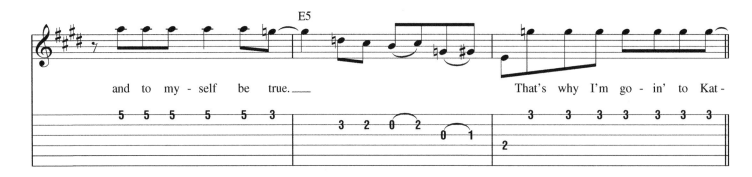

Chorus

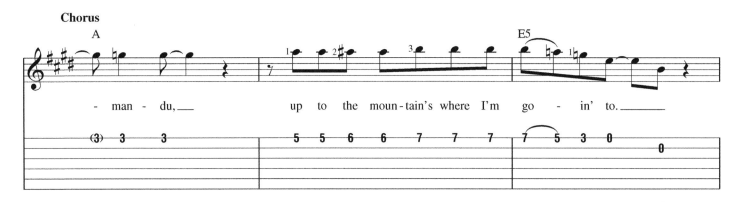

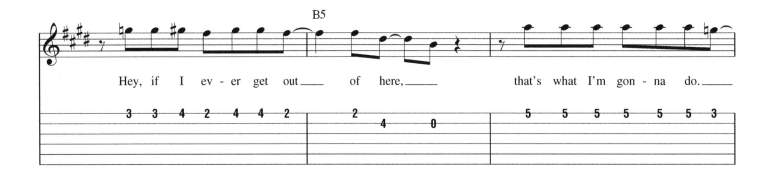

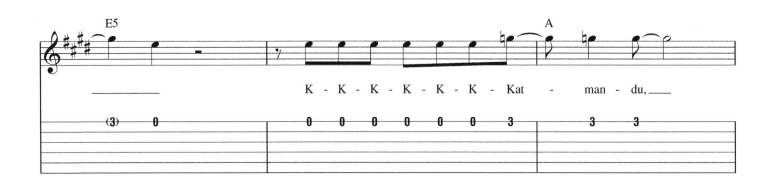

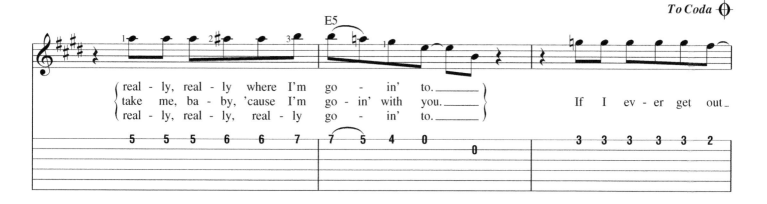

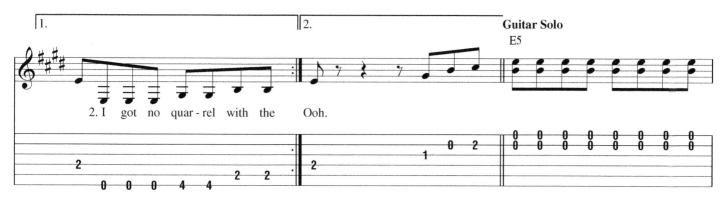

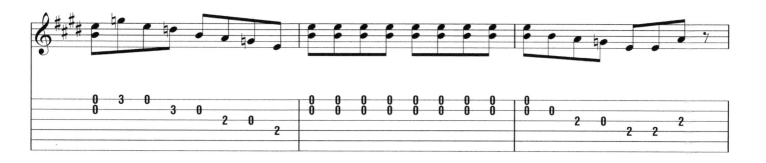

Sax Solo

D.S. al Coda

3. I ain't got noth - in' 'gainst the

Coda

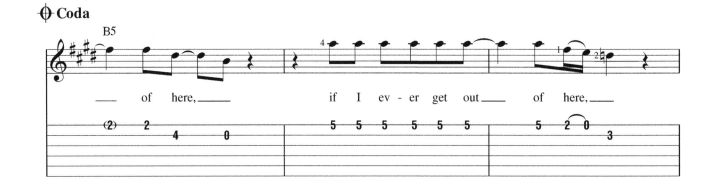

___ of here, ___ if I ev - er get out ___ of here, ___

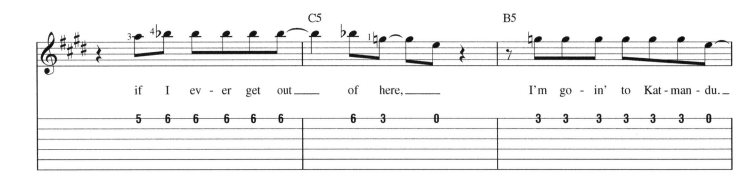

if I ev - er get out ___ of here, ___ I'm go - in' to Kat - man - du. ___

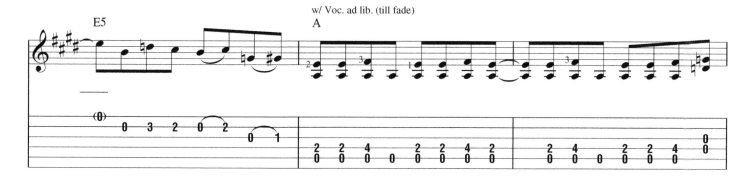

Additional Lyrics

2. I got no quarrel with the Midwest,
   The folks out there have given me their best.
   I've lived there all my life, I've been their guest,
   I sure have loved it, too.
   I'm tired of looking at the TV news,
   I'm tired of drivin' hard and payin' dues.
   I figure, baby, I've got nothin' to lose,
   I'm tired of bein' blue.

3. I ain't got nothin' 'gainst the East Coast,
   You want some people, well, they got the most.
   And New York City's like a friendly ghost,
   You seem to pass right through.
   I know I'm gonna miss the U.S.A.,
   I guess I'll miss it ev'ry single day.
   But no one loves me here anyway,
   I know my plane is due.

Mainstreet

Words and Music by Bob Seger

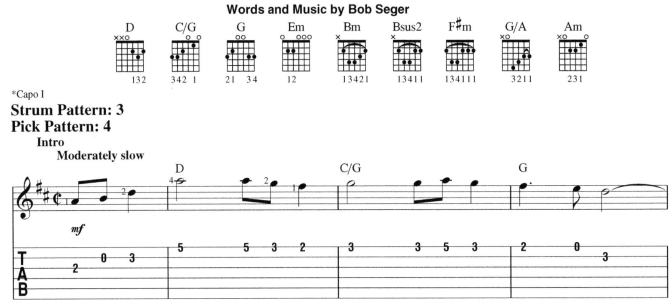

*Capo I

Strum Pattern: 3
Pick Pattern: 4

Intro
Moderately slow

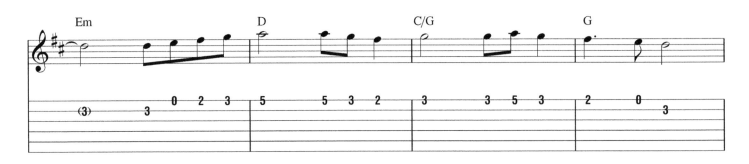

*Optional: To match recording, place capo at 1st fret.

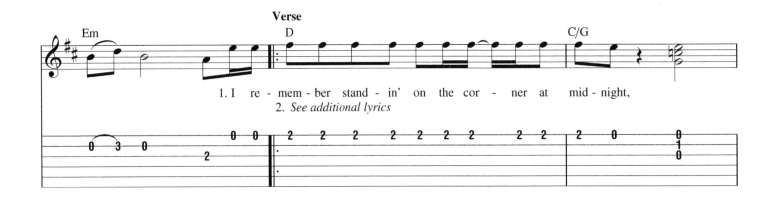

1. I re - mem - ber stand - in' on the cor - ner at mid - night,
2. *See additional lyrics*

Verse

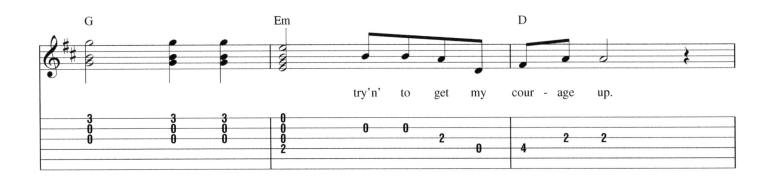

try'n' to get my cour - age up.

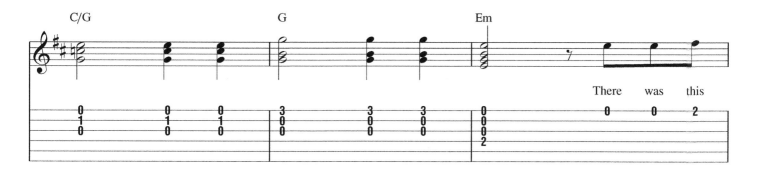

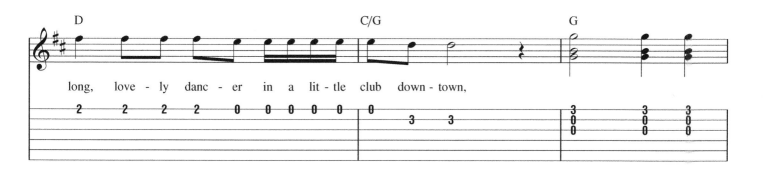

𝄋 Pre-Chorus

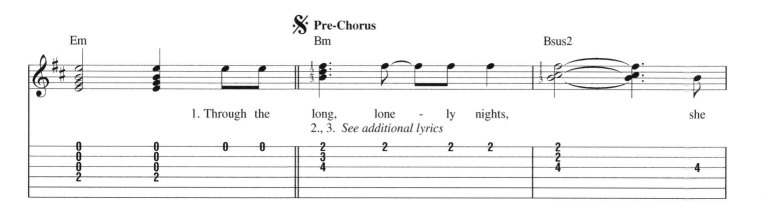

Chorus

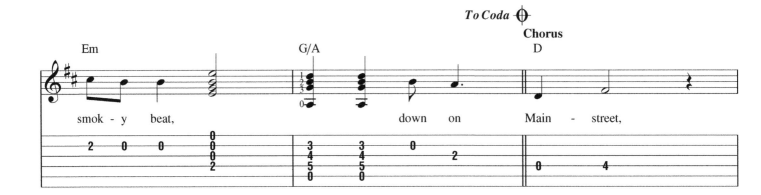

smok - y beat, down on Main - street,

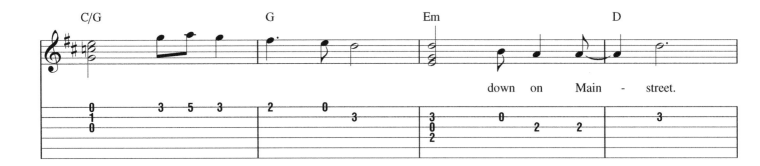

down on Main - street.

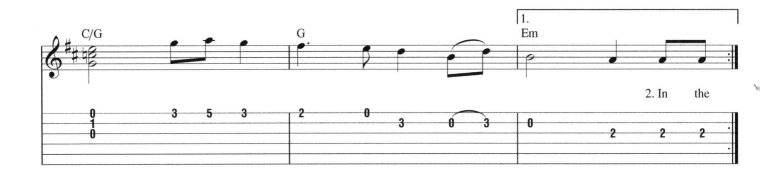

2. In the

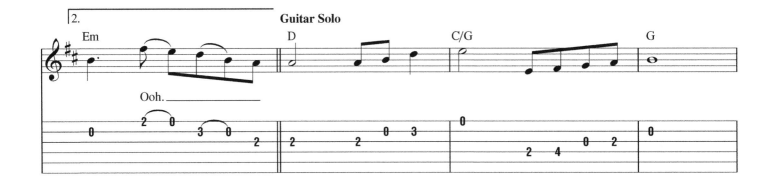

Ooh. _____

Guitar Solo

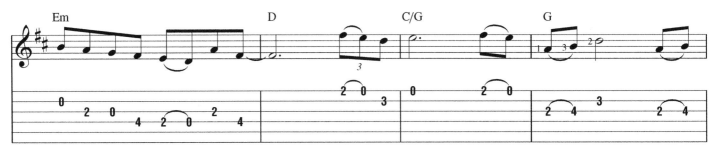

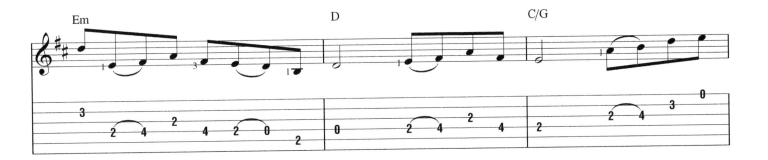

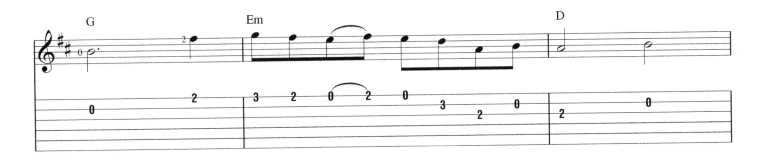

D.S. al Coda

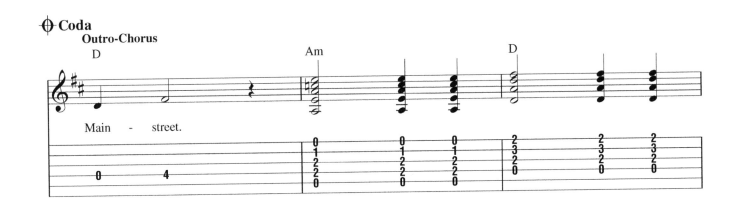

Coda
Outro-Chorus

Main - street.

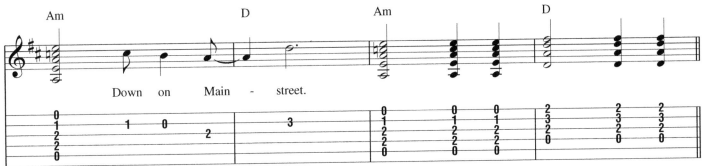

Down on Main - street.

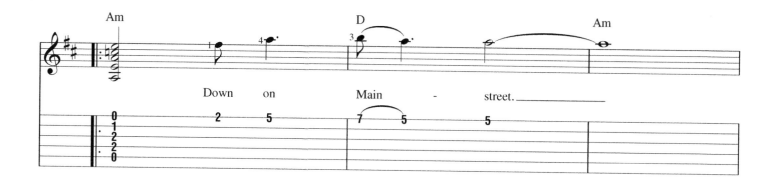

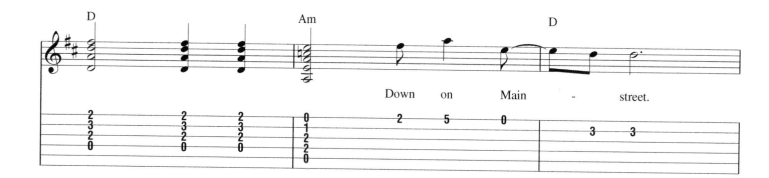

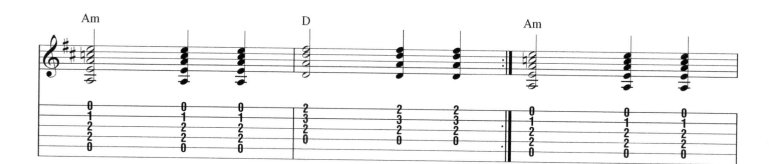

Additional Lyrics

2. In the pool halls, the hustlers and the losers,
   Used to watch 'em through the glass.
   Well, I'd stand outside at closing time,
   Just to watch her walk on past.

Pre-Chorus 2. Unlike all the other ladies,
   She looked so young and sweet,
   As she made her way alone
   Down that empty street.

Pre-Chorus 3. Sometimes even now,
   When I'm feeling lonely and beat,
   I drift back in time
   And I find my feet...

Night Moves

Words and Music by Bob Seger

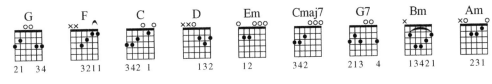

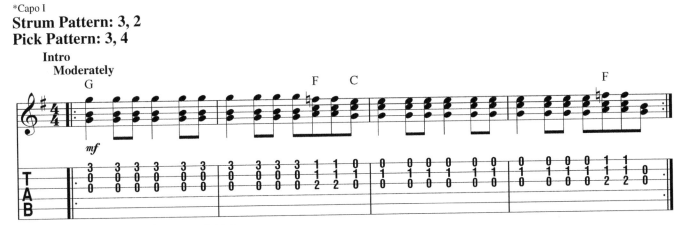

*Capo I
Strum Pattern: 3, 2
Pick Pattern: 3, 4

Intro
Moderately

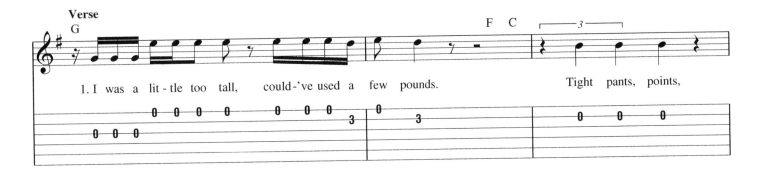

*Optional: To match recording, place capo at 1st fret.

Verse

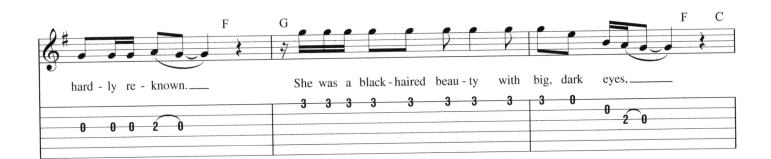

1. I was a lit-tle too tall,   could-'ve used a   few pounds.   Tight pants, points,

hard-ly re-known.___   She was a black-haired beau-ty   with big, dark eyes,___

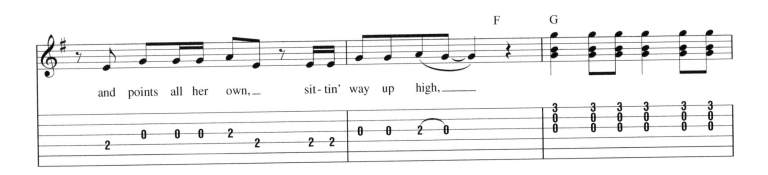

and points all her own,___   sit-tin' way up high,___

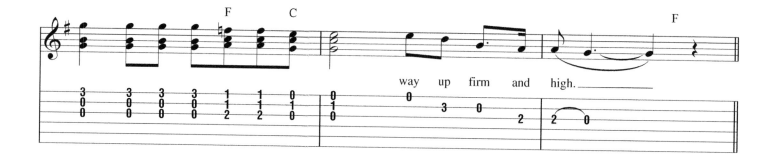

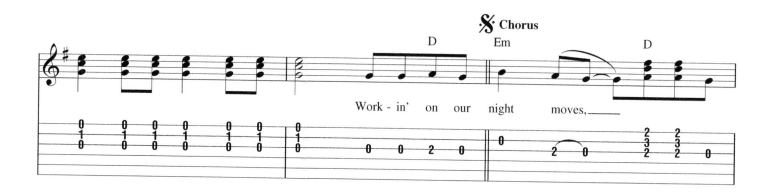

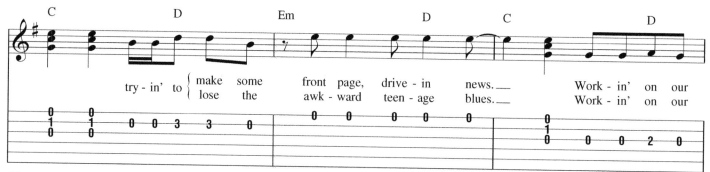

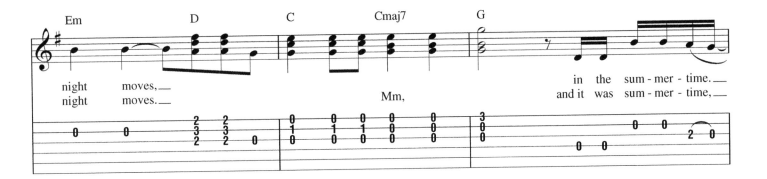

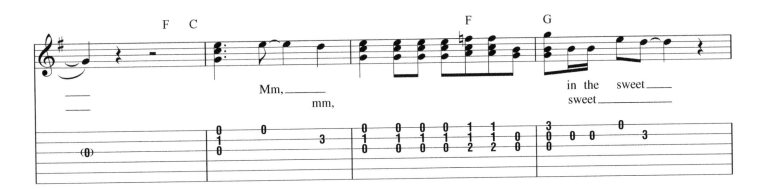

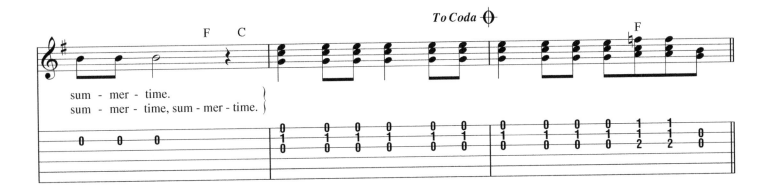

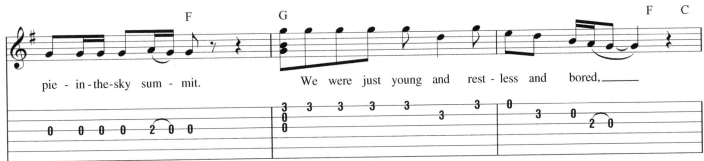

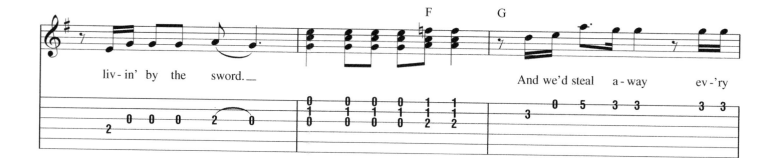

liv- in' by the sword.___ And we'd steal a- way ev-'ry

chance we could, to the back room, to the al - ley, or the trust - y woods.___

D.S. al Coda

I used her, she used me, but nei- ther one cared.___ We were get- tin' our share.___ Work- in' on our

Coda

Interlude

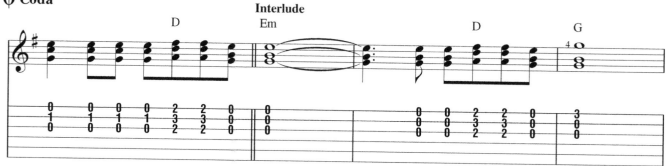

Bridge

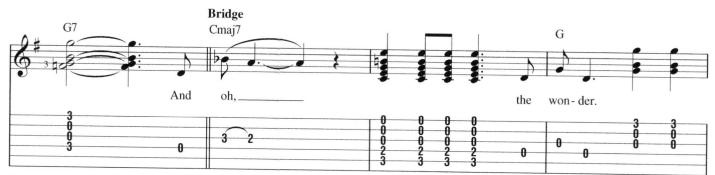

And oh,_____ the won - der.

We felt the light - ning, yeah, —

and we wait-ed on the thun - der, wait-ed on the thun - der. —

Slowly

Verse
Free time

4. I a-woke last night to the sound of thun-der. How far off, I

*One strum per chord throughout Verse

sat and won - dered. Start-ed hum-ming a song from nine - teen - six - ty two. —

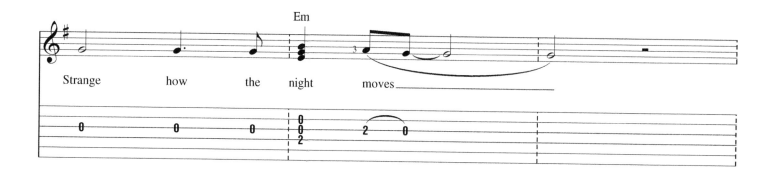

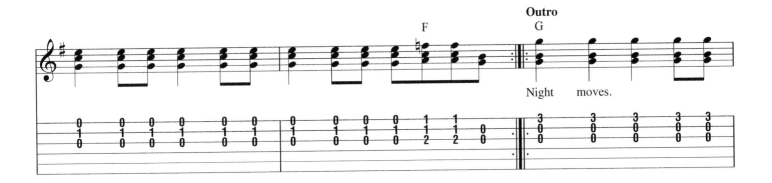

Outro

Night moves.

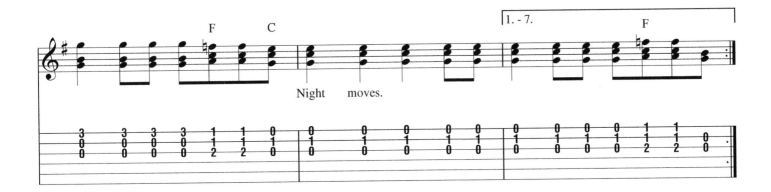

Night moves.

1. - 7.

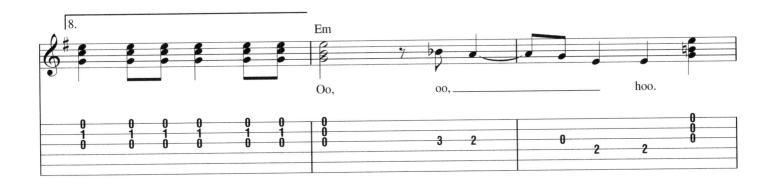

8.

Oo, oo, _____ hoo.

Oo, ah, _____ yeah, _ yeah, yeah, _ yeah. Oo, ah, _ huh.

Oo, ah, _ huh. _ Oo, I re-mem-ber, I re-mem - ber. _

Old Time Rock and Roll

Words and Music by George Jackson and Thomas E. Jones III

Strum Pattern: 5, 6

Intro
Moderate Rock

1. Just take those old rec - ords

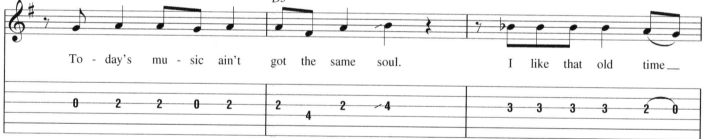

off   the   shelf. __   I'll   sit   and   lis - ten   to 'em   by   my - self. __

2. *Instrumental*
3. *See additional lyrics*

To - day's   mu - sic   ain't   got   the   same   soul.   I   like   that   old   time __

rock   'n   roll. __   Don't   try   to   take   me   to   a   dis - co.

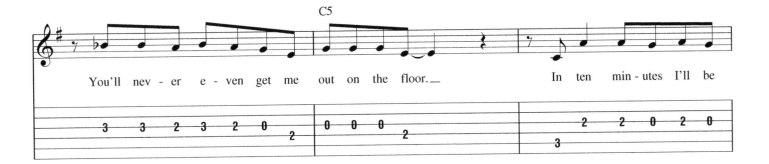

Chorus

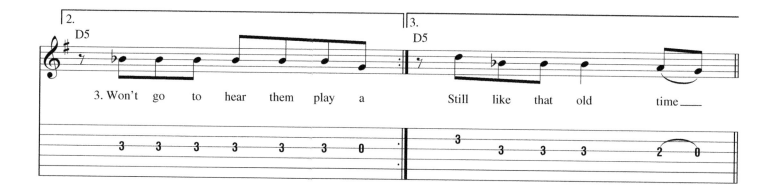

Outro-Chorus

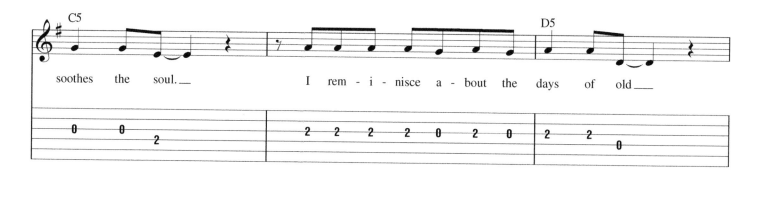

Additional Lyrics

3. Won't go to hear 'em play a tango.
   I'd rather hear some blues or funky old soul.
   There's only one sure way to get me to go:
   Start playin' old time rock 'n roll.
   Call me a relic, call me what you will.
   Say I'm old-fashioned, say I'm over the hill.
   Today's music ain't got the same soul.
   I like that old time rock 'n roll.

Roll Me Away

Words and Music by Bob Seger

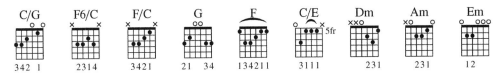

Strum Pattern: 2, 6
Pick Pattern: 4, 5

Intro
Moderately fast

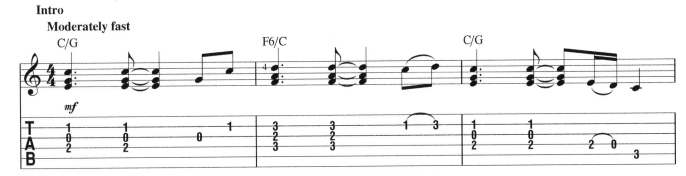

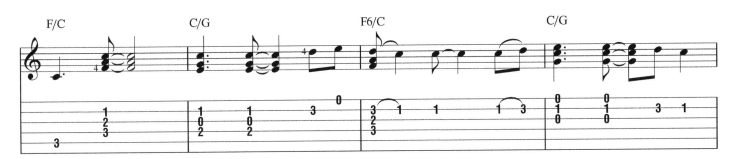

1. Took a look down a west-bound road,___ right a-
2. Twelve___ hours out of Mack-in-aw Cit-y, stopped at a
3. *See additional lyrics*

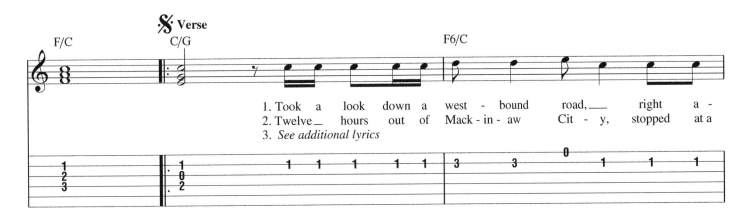

way I made my choice.___
bar to have a brew.___

Head-ed out to my
Met a girl and we

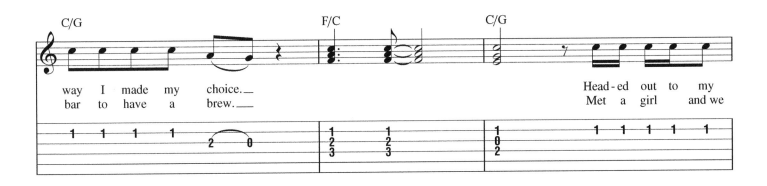

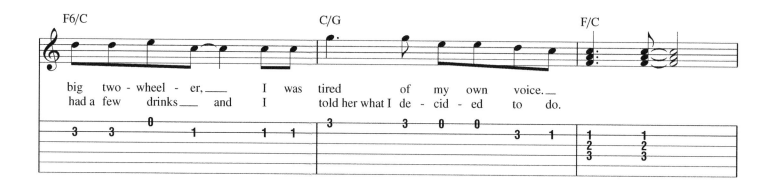

big two - wheel - er, __ I was tired of my own voice. __
had a few drinks __ and I told her what I de - cid - ed to do.

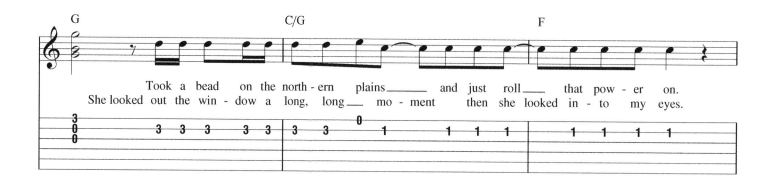

Took a bead on the north - ern plains __ and just roll __ that pow - er on.
She looked out the win - dow a long, long __ mo - ment then she looked in - to my eyes.

1.
She did - n't have to say a thing,

2.

Chorus

I knew what she was think - in.'

Roll, roll me a - way, won't you
Roll, roll me a - way, I'm gon - na

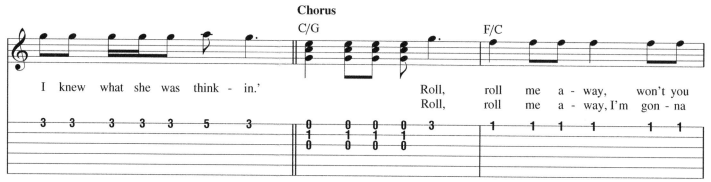

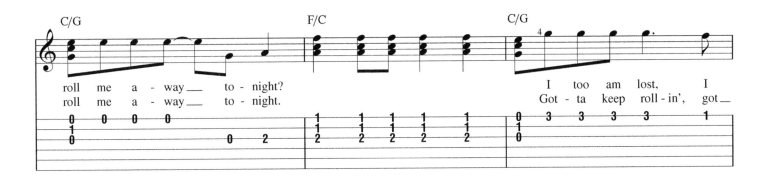

roll me a - way___ to - night?
roll me a - way___ to - night.

I too am lost, I
Got - ta keep roll - in', got ___

feel doub - le - crossed and I'm sick of what's wrong___ and what's
___ to keep rid - in' keep search - in' til I find___ what's___

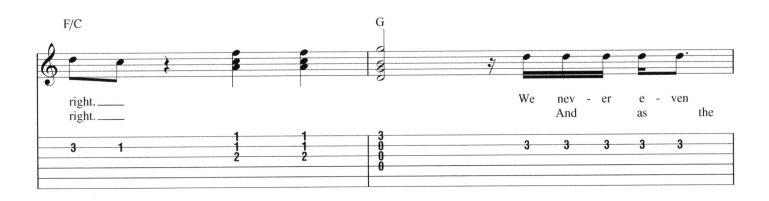

right.___
right.___

We nev - er e - ven
And as the

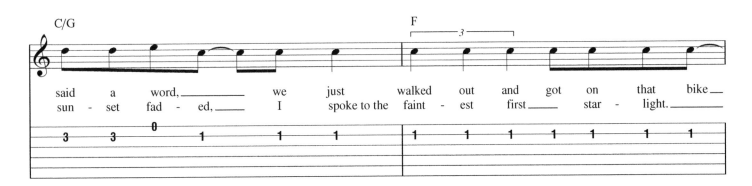

said a word,___ we just walked out and got on that bike___
sun - set fad - ed,___ I spoke to the faint - est first___ star - light.___

To Coda ⊕

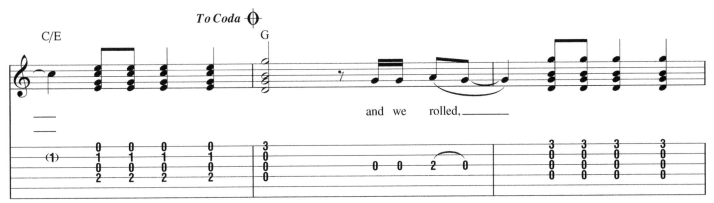

and we rolled,___

and we rolled clean out a sight.

Interlude

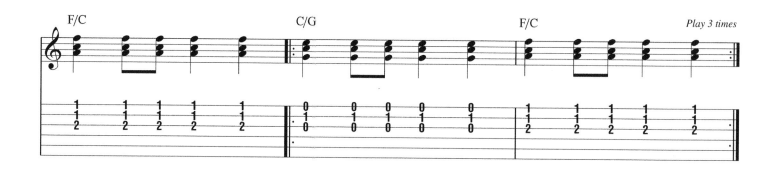

Bridge

We rolled __ a-cross the high plains, __ deep __ in-to the
Some-where __ a-long the high road, __ the air __ be-gan to

moun - tains. __ It felt so good to me,
turn cold. __ She said she missed her home,

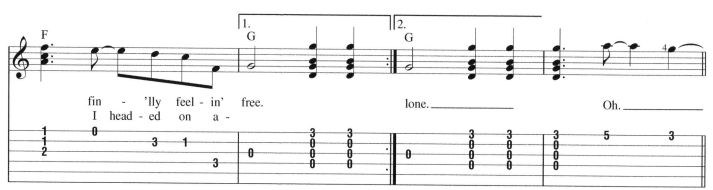

fin - 'lly feel-in' free. lone. __
I head-ed on a- Oh. __

Interlude

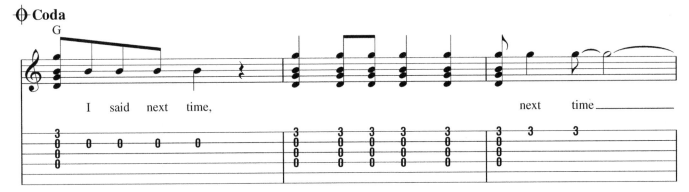

I said next time, next time_____

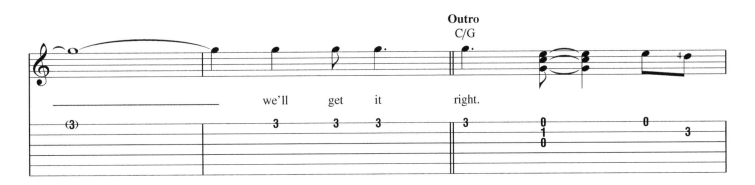

_____ we'll get it right.

Additional Lyrics

3. Stood alone on a mountain top,
   Starin' out at the Great Divide.
   I could go east, I could go west,
   It was all up to me to decide.
   Just then I saw a young hawk flyin'
   And my soul began to rise.
   And pretty soon
   My heart was singin'.

The Real Love

Words and Music by Bob Seger

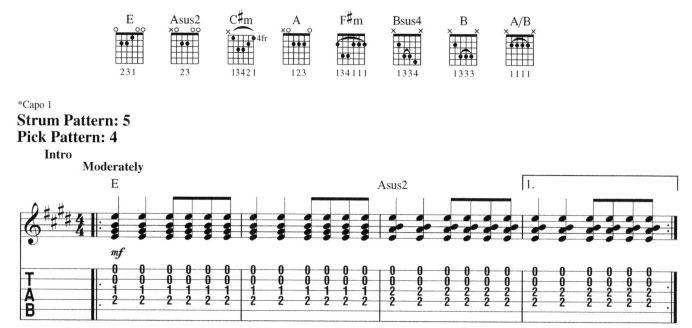

E   Asus2   C#m   A   F#m   Bsus4   B   A/B

*Capo 1

Strum Pattern: 5

Pick Pattern: 4

Intro

Moderately

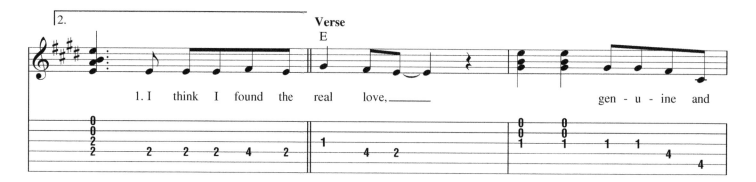

*Optional: To match recording, place capo at 1st fret.

1. I think I found the real love,_____ gen - u - ine and

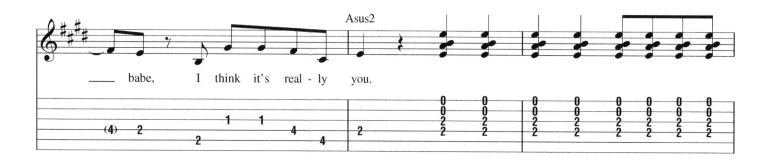

true.   I think it's real - ly come my way__ to - day,__

_____ babe, I think it's real - ly you.

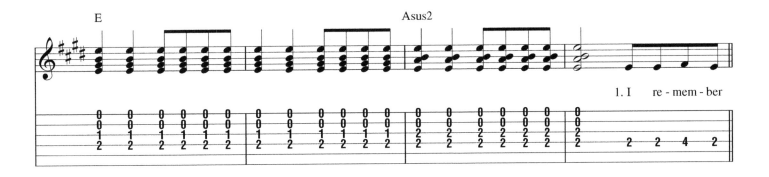

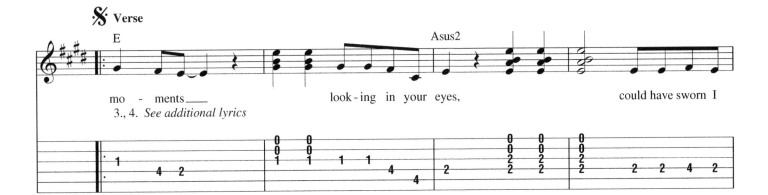

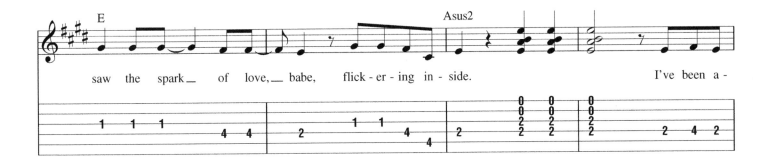

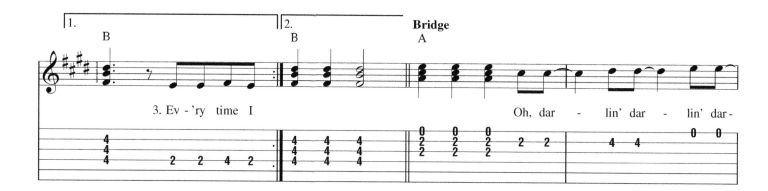

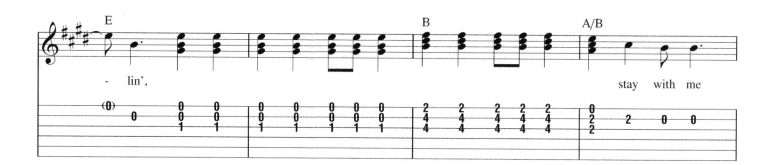

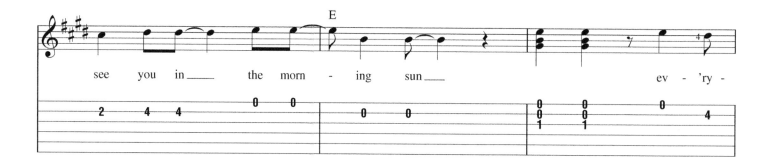

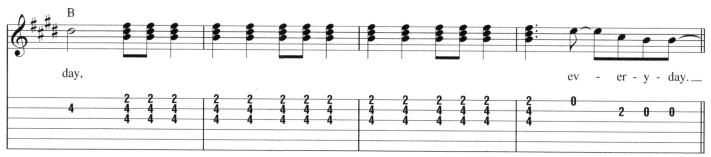

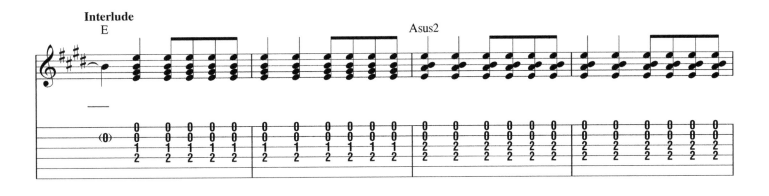

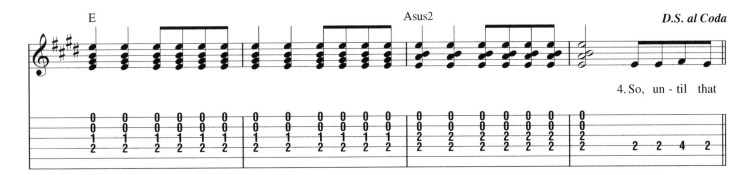

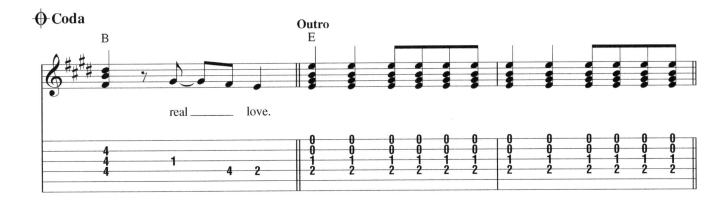

Additional Lyrics

3. Every time I see you, ev'ry time we touch,
   I can feel the way you feel for me, babe, and it means so much.
   And ev'ry time you look at me,
   It's just the way it all should be
   In the real love.

4. So, until that moment when I take your hand,
   Gonna try to do my very best, babe, to prove that I'm your man.
   I'm gonna do my very best,
   I'm not gonna rest
   Until we've got the real love, real love.

Rock and Roll Never Forgets

Words and Music by Bob Seger

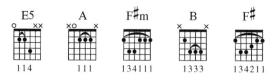

Strum Pattern: 2, 3

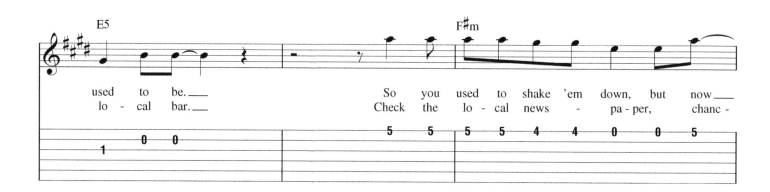

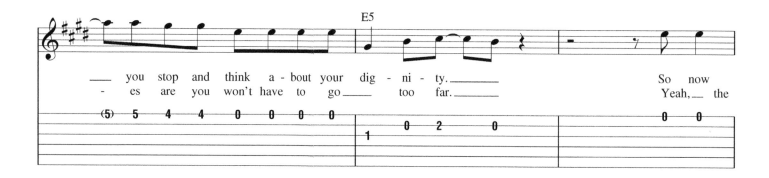

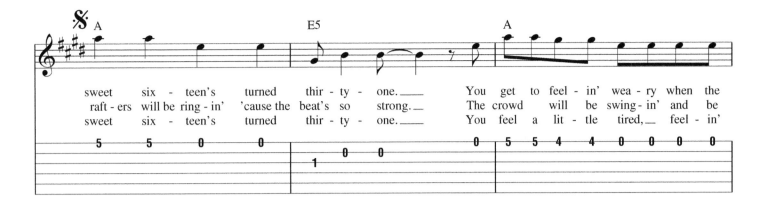

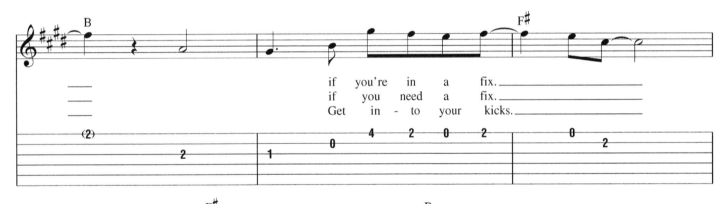

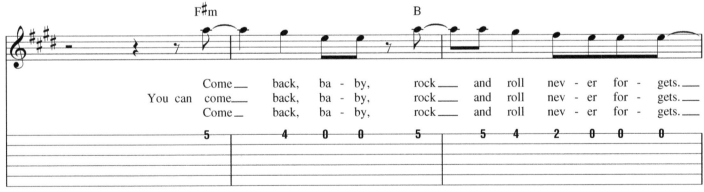

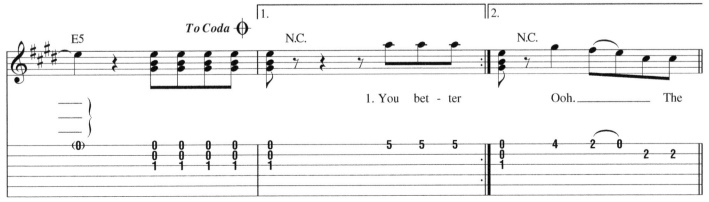

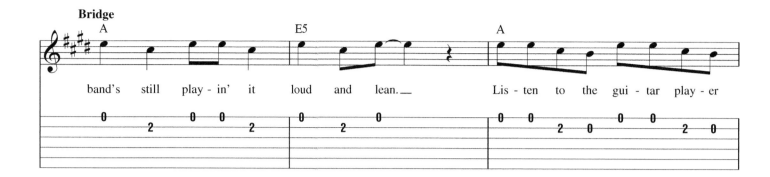

band's still play - in' it loud and lean.___ Lis - ten to the gui - tar play - er

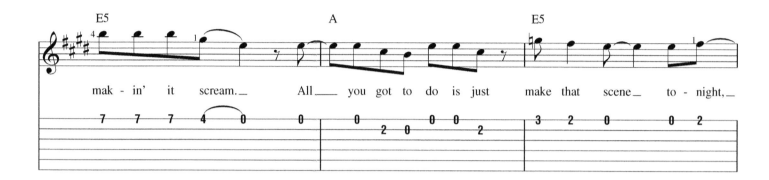

mak - in' it scream.___ All___ you got to do is just make that scene___ to - night,

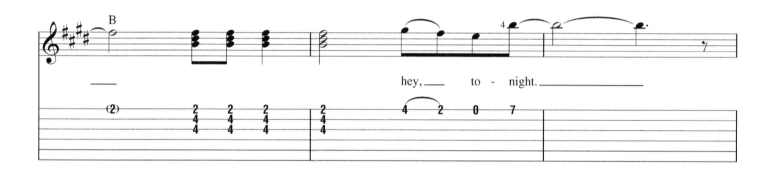

___ hey,___ to - night.___

Guitar Solo

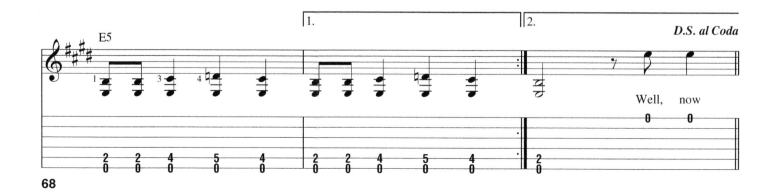

Well, now

Coda

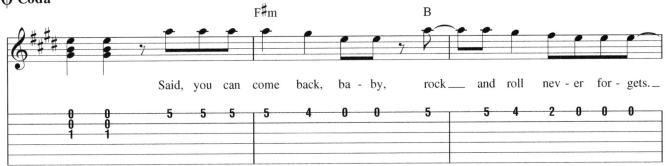

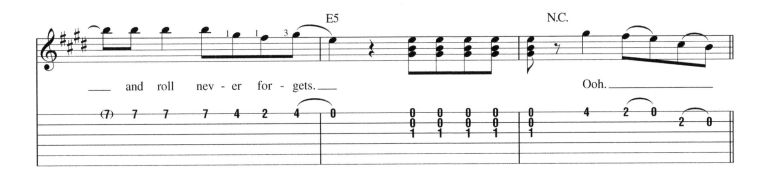

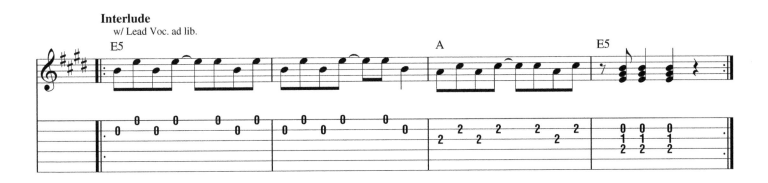

Interlude
w/ Lead Voc. ad lib.

Outro
w/ Lead Voc. ad lib.

Repeat and fade

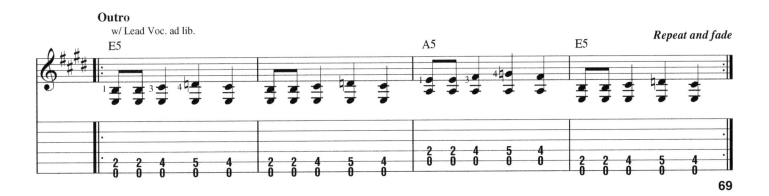

Still the Same

Words and Music by Bob Seger

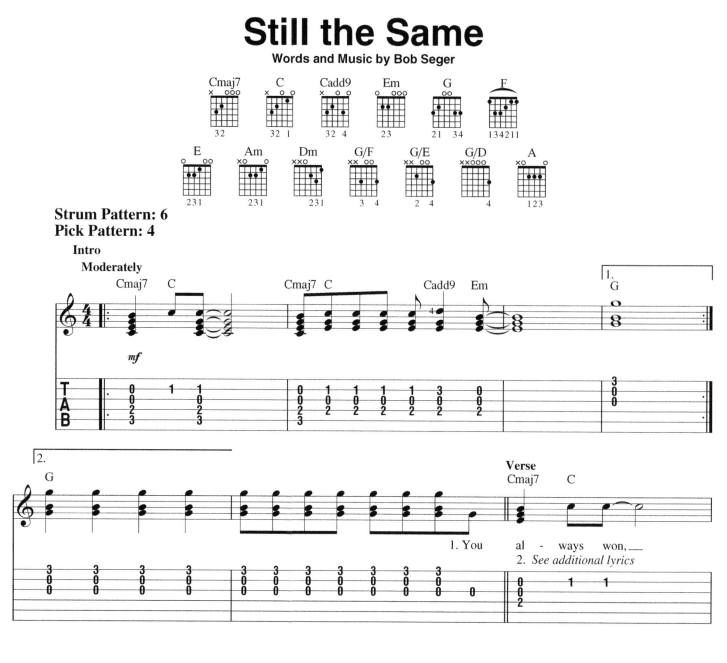

Strum Pattern: 6
Pick Pattern: 4

Intro
Moderately

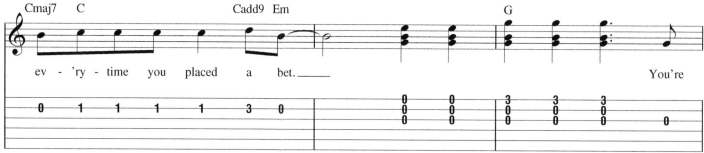

1. You al - ways won, ___
2. *See additional lyrics*

ev - 'ry - time you placed a bet. ___

You're

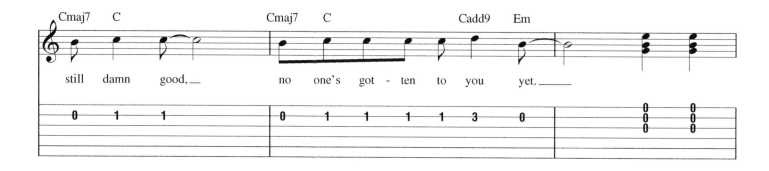

still damn good, ___ no one's got - ten to you yet. ___

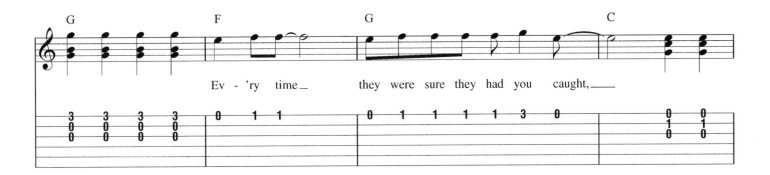

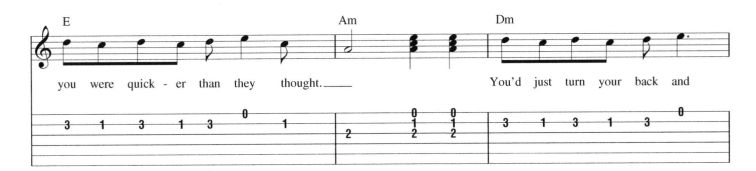

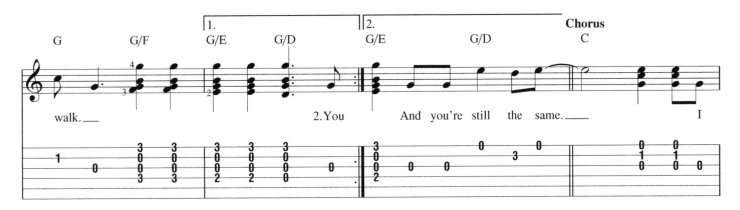

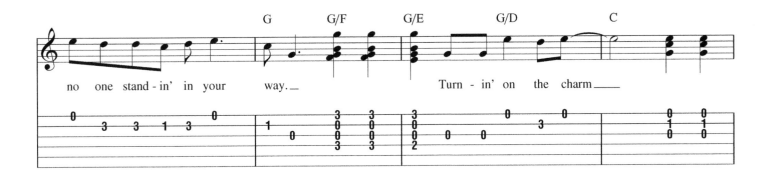

long e-nough to get you by. ____   You're still the same. ____

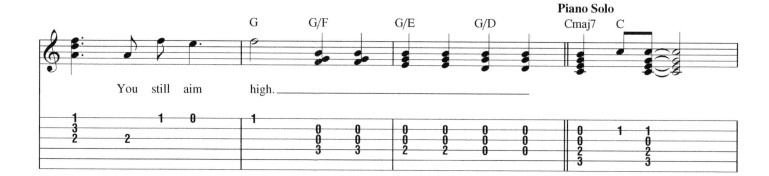

Piano Solo

You still aim high. ____

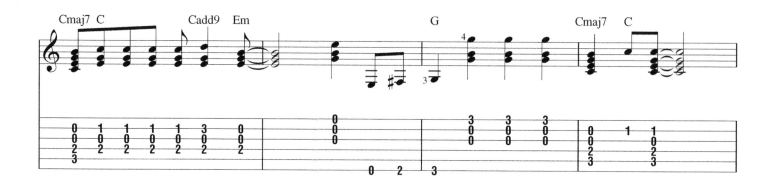

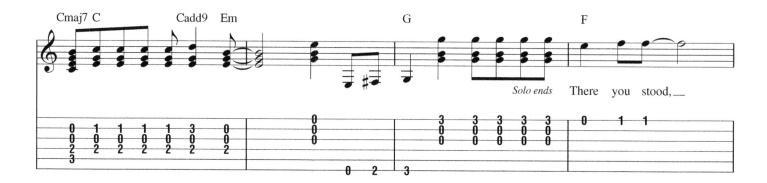

Solo ends There you stood, ____

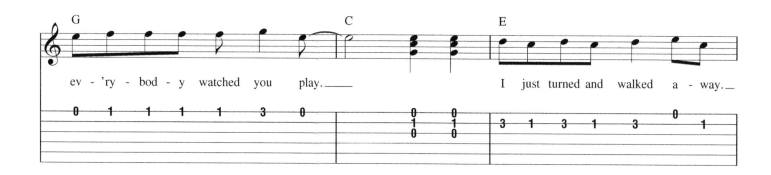

ev-'ry-bod-y watched you play. ____   I just turned and walked a-way. ____

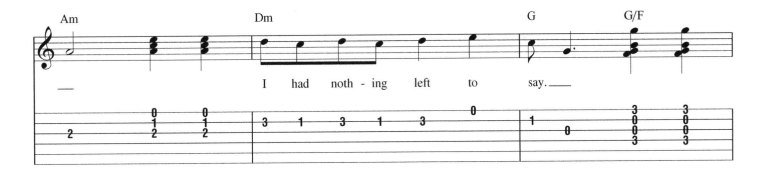

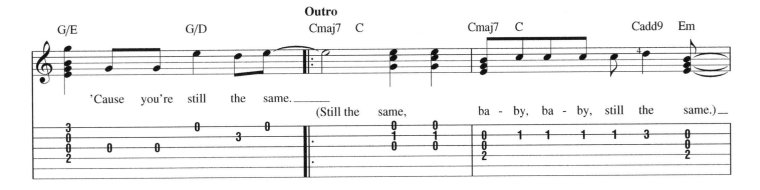

Additional Lyrics

2. You always said, the cards would never do you wrong.
The trick, you said, was never play the game too long.
A gambler's share, the only risk that you would take,
The only loss you could forsake,
The only bluff you couldn't fake.

Turn the Page

Words and Music by Bob Seger

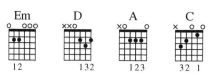

Strum Pattern: 4
Pick Pattern: 5

Intro
Moderately slow

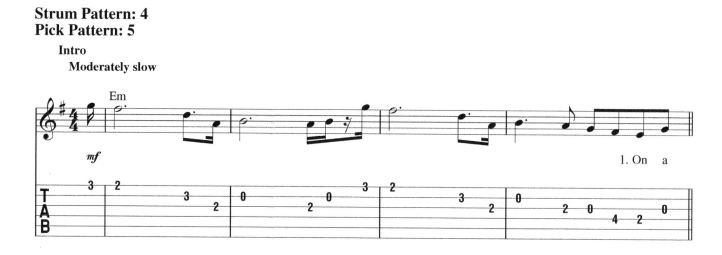

1. On a

Verse

long and lone-some high-way,_____ east of O - ma - ha,_____ you can
3. *See additional lyrics*

lis-ten to the en - gine moan-in' out his one note song. You can

think a-bout__ the wom - an,___ or the girl you knew the night__ be - fore.___

2. But your thoughts will soon be wan - der - ing,___ the way they al - ways do,___ when you're
4., 5. *See additional lyrics*

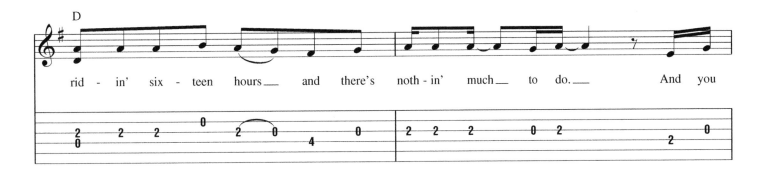

rid - in' six - teen hours___ and there's noth - in' much___ to do.___ And you

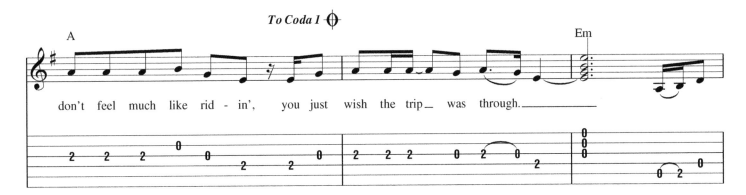

don't feel much like rid - in', you just wish the trip___ was through._____

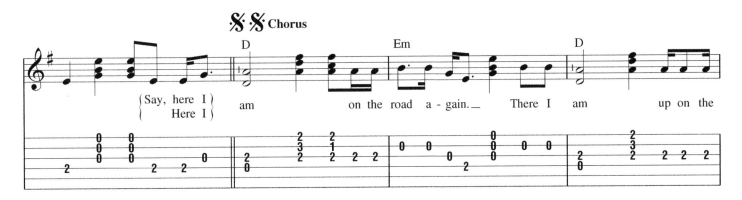

(Say, here I) am on the road a - gain.___ There I am up on the
(Here I)

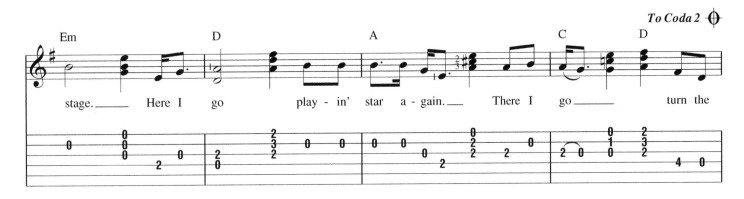

stage.____ Here I go play - in' star a - gain.___ There I go___ turn the

3. Well, you

D.S. al Coda 1

Coda 1

mu - sic that you play._____

6. Lat - er in the eve - ning as you

*One strum per chord, next 8 meas.

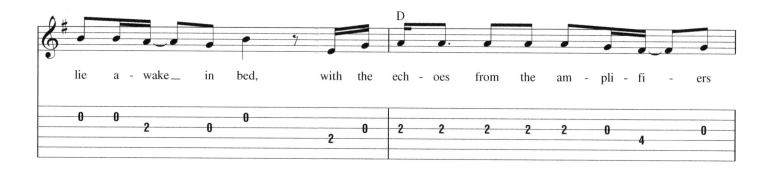

lie a - wake__ in bed, with the ech - oes from the am - pli - fi - ers

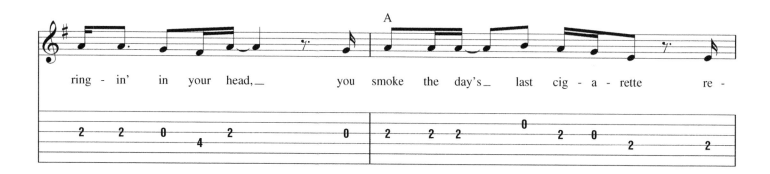

ring - in' in your head,__ you smoke the day's__ last cig - a - rette re -

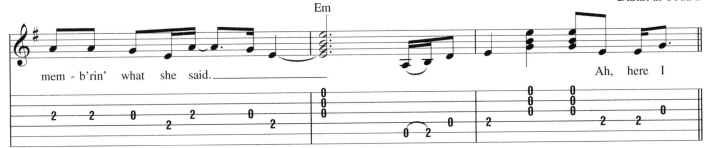

mem - b'rin' what she said._____ Ah, here I

Coda 2

Outro-Chorus

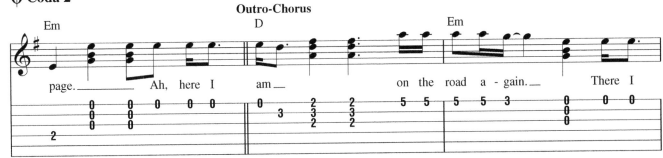

page._____ Ah, here I am ___ on the road a - gain. ___ There I

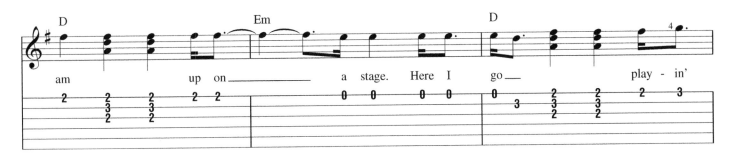

am up on _____ a stage. Here I go ___ play - in'

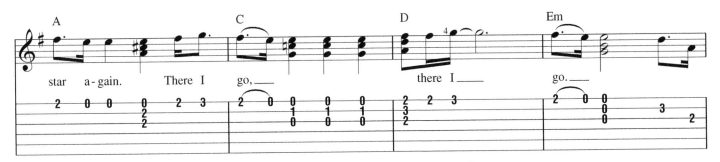

star a - gain. There I go, ___ there I ___ go. ___

rit.

Additional Lyrics

3. Well, you walk into a restaurant, strung out from the road,
   And you feel the eyes upon you as you're shakin' off the cold,
   You pretend it doesn't bother you, but you just want to explode.

4. Most times you can't hear 'em talk, other times you can.
   All the same old clichés, "Is that a woman or a man?"
   And you always seem outnumbered, you don't dare make a stand.

5. Out there in the spotlight, you're a million miles away,
   Every ounce of energy, you try to give away,
   As the sweat pours out your body like the music that you play.

You'll Accomp'ny Me

Words and Music by Bob Seger

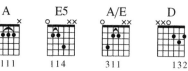

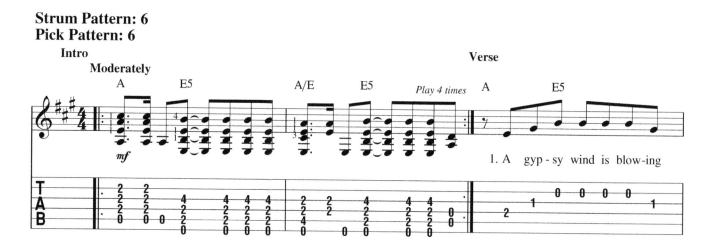

Strum Pattern: 6
Pick Pattern: 6

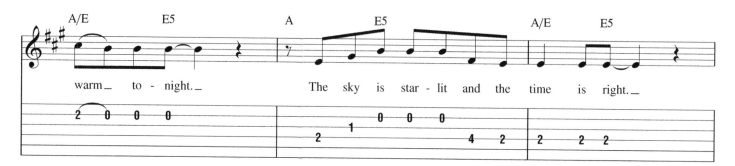

1. A gyp-sy wind is blow-ing

warm_ to - night._ The sky is star-lit and the time is right._

And still you're tell-in' me you have_ to go. Be - fore you leave there's some-thing

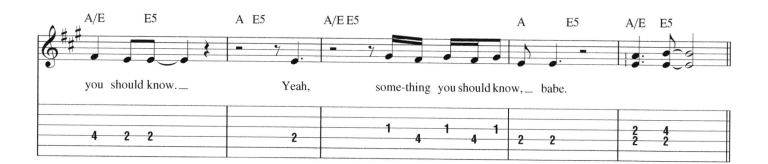

you should know._ Yeah, some-thing you should know,_ babe.

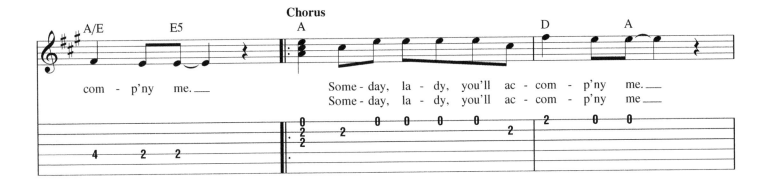

Chorus

com - p'ny me. ___

Some - day, la - dy, you'll ac - com - p'ny me. __
Some - day, la - dy, you'll ac - com - p'ny me __

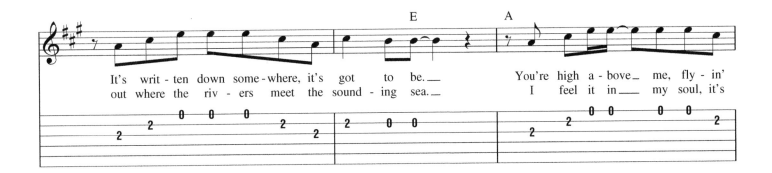

It's writ - ten down some - where, it's got to be. __
out where the riv - ers meet the sound - ing sea. __

You're high a - bove __ me, fly - in'
I feel it in __ my soul, it's

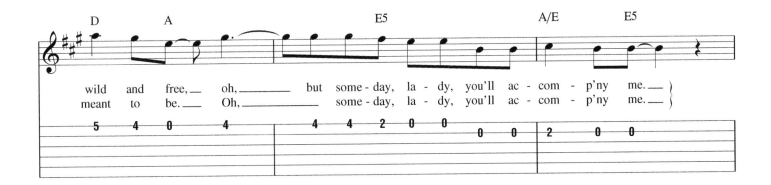

wild and free, __ oh, _____ but some - day, la - dy, you'll ac - com - p'ny me. __)
meant to be. __ Oh, _____ some - day, la - dy, you'll ac - com - p'ny me. __ }

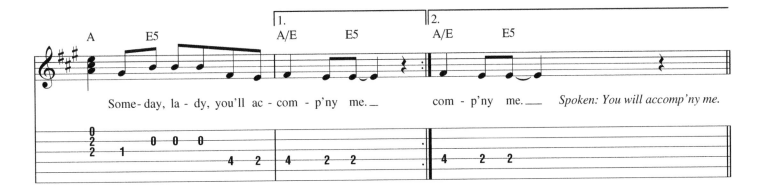

1.

Some - day, la - dy, you'll ac - com - p'ny me. __

2.

com - p'ny me. __ *Spoken: You will accomp'ny me.*

Outro
w/ Lead Voc. ad lib.

Repeat and fade

(Oo, hoo. __

Oo, hoo, __ you'll ac - com - p'ny me.) __

We've Got Tonight

Words and Music by Bob Seger

*Capo II

Strum Pattern: 3, 4
Pick Pattern: 5

Intro
Slowly

*Optional: To match recording, place capo at 2nd fret.

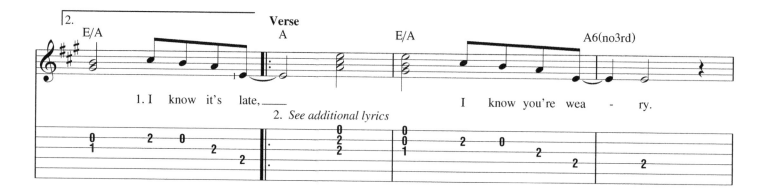

Verse

1. I know it's late,___ I know you're wea - ry.

2. *See additional lyrics*

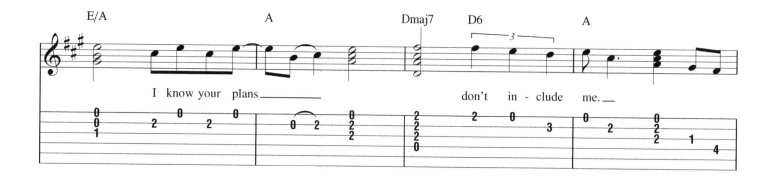

I know your plans___ don't in - clude me.___

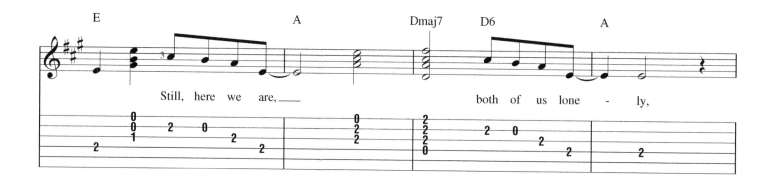

Still, here we are,___ both of us lone - ly,

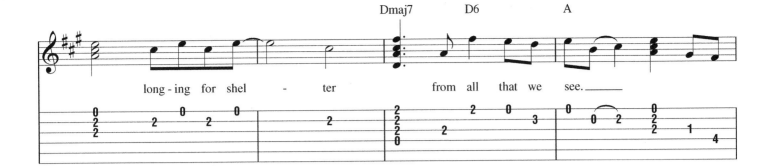

long-ing for shel - ter ... from all that we see.___

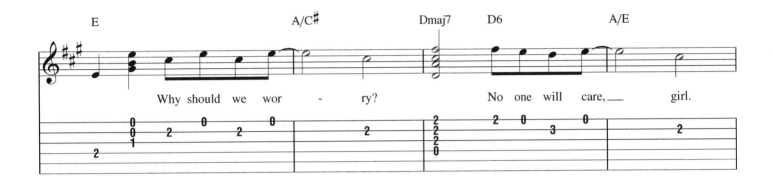

Why should we wor - ry? ... No one will care,___ girl.

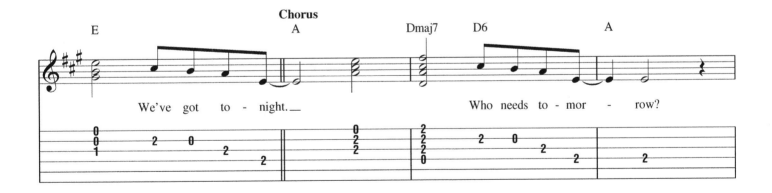

Look at the stars___ ... so far a - way.___

Chorus

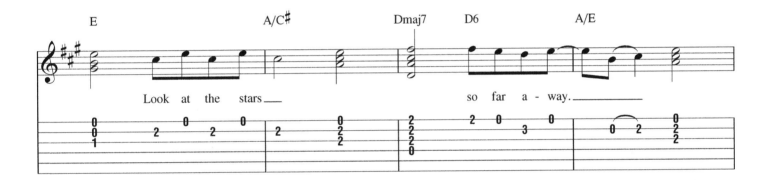

We've got to - night.___ ... Who needs to - mor - row?

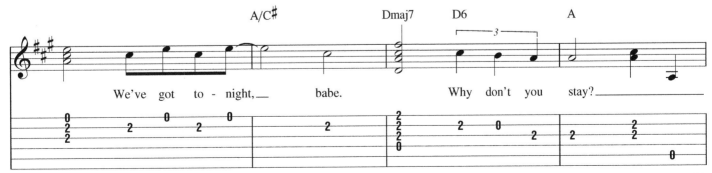

We've got to - night,___ babe. ... Why don't you stay?___

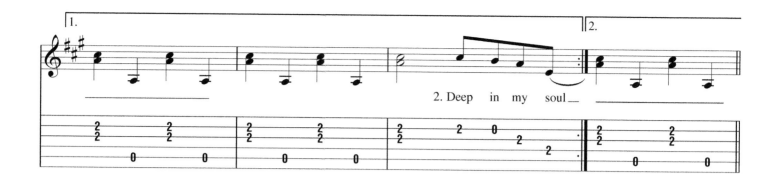

Bridge

I know it's late, I know you're wea - ry.

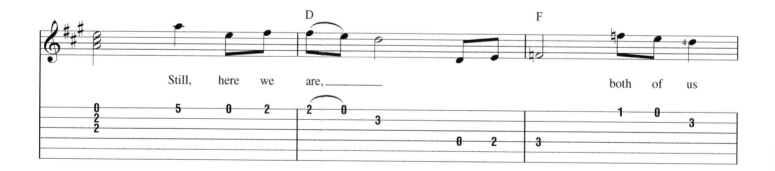

Ooh, _____ I know your plans don't in - clude me.

Still, here we are, _____ both of us

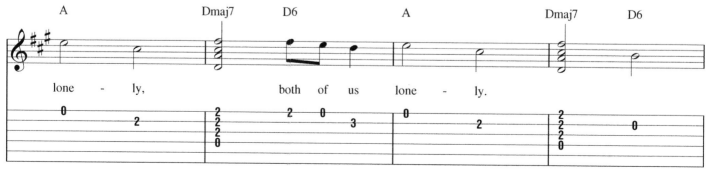

lone - ly, both of us lone - ly.

We've got to - night.____

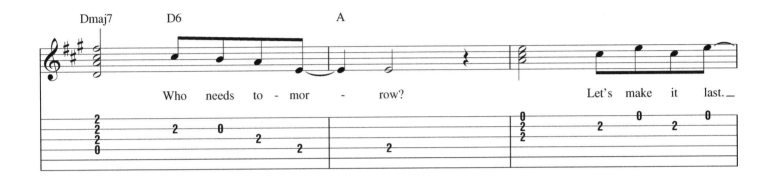

Who needs to - mor - row? Let's make it last.__

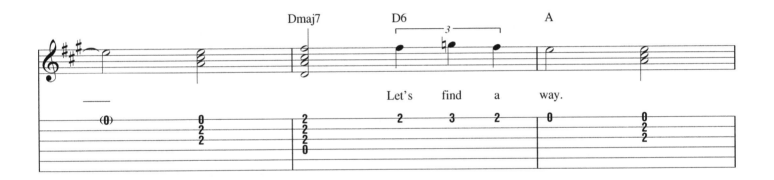

Let's find a way.

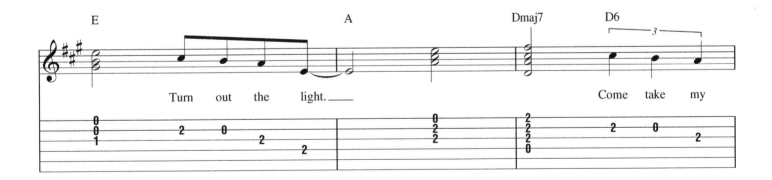

Turn out the light.____ Come take my

hand now. We've got to - night,____ babe.

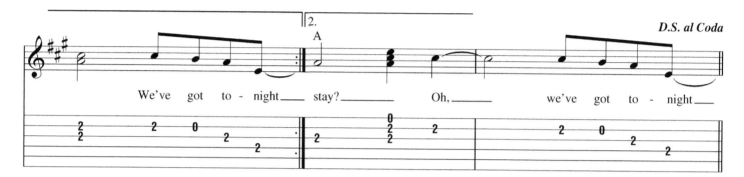

 Coda

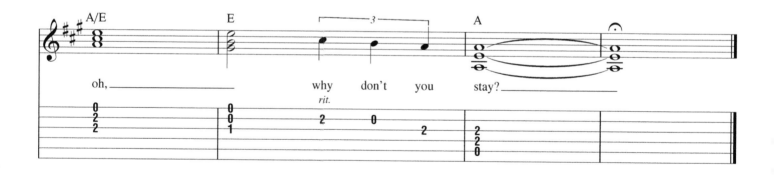

Additional Lyrics

2. Deep in my soul I've been so lonely,
   All of my hopes fading away.
   I've longed for love like everyone else does.
   I know I'll keep searching even after today.
   So there it is, girl. I've said it all now.
   And here we are, babe. What do you say?